WHAT TEACHING
LOOKS LIKE

Center for Engaged Learning
Open Access Book Series

Series editors, Jessie L. Moore and Peter Felten

The Center for Engaged Learning (CEL) Open Access Book Series features concise, peer-reviewed books (both authored books and edited collections) for a multi-disciplinary, international, higher education audience interested in research-informed engaged learning practices.

The CEL Open Access Book Series offers an alternate publishing option for high-quality engaged learning books that align with the Center's mission, goals, and initiatives, and that experiment with genre or medium in ways that take advantage of an online and open access format.

CEL is committed to making these publications freely available to a global audience.

Pedagogical Partnerships: A How-To Guide for Faculty, Students, and Academic Developers in Higher Education
Alison Cook-Sather, Melanie Bahti, and Anita Ntem
https://doi.org/10.36284/celelon.oa1

The Power of Partnership: Students, Staff, and Faculty Revolutionizing Higher Education
Edited by Lucy Mercer-Mapstone and Sophia Abbot
https://doi.org/10.36284/celelon.oa2

Writing about Learning and Teaching in Higher Education: Creating and Contributing to Scholarly Conversations across a Range of Genres
Mick Healey, Kelly E. Matthews, and Alison Cook-Sather
https://doi.org/10.36284/celelon.oa3

What Teaching Looks Like

Higher Education through Photographs

_____

Cassandra Volpe Horii and Martin Springborg

Elon University Center for Engaged Learning
Elon, North Carolina
www.CenterForEngagedLearning.org

Series editors: Jessie L. Moore and Peter Felten
Copyeditor and designer: Jennie Goforth

Cataloging-in-Publication Data
Names: Horii, Cassandra Volpe | Springborg, Martin
Title: What Teaching Looks Like: Higher Education through Photographs / Cassandra Volpe Horii and Martin Springborg
Description: Elon, North Carolina : Elon University Center for Engaged Learning, [2022] | Series: Center for Engaged Learning open access book series | Includes bibliographical references and index.
Identifiers: LCCN 2022939540 | ISBN (PDF) 978-1-951414-07-8 | ISBN (pbk.) 978-1-951414-06-1 | DOI https://doi.org/10.36284/celelon.oa4
Subjects: LCSH: College teaching – Pictorial works | College teachers – Pictorial works

DEDICATION

Again, for Emma. And for Henry, McKenna, and Lexi.
May you all find the learning you need.
—MS

In memory of Mom and Dad, who taught me to love learning;
for Maya—I hope you always will.
—CVH

The photographs are not illustrative. They, and the text, are coequal, mutually independent, and fully collaborative.

—*James Agee*

ACKNOWLEDGMENTS

We are deeply grateful to every one of the campuses that hosted *The Teaching and Learning Project*; their institutional leaders welcomed this new and somewhat unknown photographic project and the transformations it would spark. At the completion of this book, campus hosts include multiple colleges and campuses within the Minnesota State system, the California Institute of Technology (Caltech), Marquette University, multiple colleges and campuses within the Pennsylvania State system (Penn State), Elon University, Cornell University, the University of Virginia, the University of Michigan, Wayne State University, Texas Tech University, Brown University, Princeton University, and Saint Louis University. We thank the faculty, students, staff, and administrators who agreed to be included in the project on each of those campuses.

Our thanks go to every one of the individual faculty members we have worked with in our capacities as educational developers. Whether as newly appointed tenure-track assistant professors, tenured professors with decades of experience, part-time or full-time lecturers, or in other types of faculty appointments, these faculty members have typically taken it upon themselves to engage in opportunities to discuss and improve their teaching, evincing over and over again their dedication to their students and to the purposes of postsecondary education. It is a true privilege to walk alongside our colleagues as they grapple with the large and small questions of what it means to teach, and how to do so well.

We have been lucky to work with undergraduate and graduate students in a variety of ways during our careers as educational developers and faculty members ourselves—in photography, design, undergraduate writing, science, and engineering courses; in graduate courses on pedagogy; and in their roles as teaching assistants, student leaders, and advisees. Our thanks go to our students over the years for their willingness to risk learning deeply, for their excellent questions, and for making us more thoughtful teachers.

Our community of educational developers and higher education change agents is beyond phenomenal. Through the POD Network in Higher Education, which first brought us together, and organizations with foci ranging from regional accreditation to national higher education and STEM education reform, we have both found inspiration, encouragement, good challenges, deep learning, and friendship. We developed many of the ideas in this book through conference sessions, coffee break discussions, and other interactions with this community over the past decade. Special thanks to Gary Hawkins, Mathew Ouellett, Suzanne Tapp, Shaun Longstreet, Deandra Little, Mary Wright, Angela Linse, Michael Palmer, Natasha Haugnes, C. Edward Watson, and James Lang, who all believed in this project.

Throughout the writing of this book, like so many people during the especially challenging period surrounding the years 2020 and 2021, we've navigated major family changes, illnesses, and deaths; a global pandemic; and personal challenges too big to name here. For us both, it has been a source of inspiration and hope to continue our collaboration through our work on this volume; we share profound gratitude for one another's friendship. We express deep sympathy to all who have lost loved ones during the COVID-19 pandemic and gratitude to all the healthcare and frontline workers who risked their lives to help others during this time.

Bigtime thanks go to our families. Like, more than we know how to say. Not just for tolerating our sometimes absences while working on the book, through odd moments and dedicated days, but for believing in us and encouraging us to share and challenge ourselves.

Cassandra: Thank you, Michael and Maya, for understanding me more than anyone and being yourselves completely. Chris, Kathy, and Sophie, thank you for your love and support. The curiosity, problem-solving, humor, and aesthetic appreciation it took to create this book are gifts from my mom and dad, Nancy and Chester Volpe; I am grateful always for their gifts and the time we had together.

Martin: Thank you, Sarah, for your patience and understanding as I "became one with" this book, and for accepting the many evenings of parallel book writing/show streaming time we spent on the couch. Mom, Dad, and Marilyn: thank you for supporting me in every way you could as I went off to college. The experience changed my life in ways I never could have dreamed.

Finally, our appreciation goes to the Center for Engaged Learning at Elon University for creating the Open Access Book Series and bringing scholarship on engaged learning to an international readership, with profound commitments to access, inclusion, and dialogue. We are grateful for the thoughtful editorial input of series editors, Jessie Moore and Peter Felten, and managing editor, Jennie Goforth.

CONTENTS

Introduction: The Origins of The Teaching and Learning Project   1

Chapter 1: Classroom Interactions   43
The Heart of Teaching and Learning

Chapter 2: Student Perspectives   81
Views from the Back of the Class and Elsewhere

Chapter 3: Productive Chaos   119
The Messy Nature of Education

Chapter 4: The Physical and Technological Environment   151
The Where and How of Teaching

Chapter 5: Beyond Campus   197
Teaching and Learning in Context

Chapter 6: Hidden Work   227
Educational Labor Revealed

Chapter 7: Photographs and Change Agents   269
Campus Communities Encountering Themselves

0.01
*A faculty member in mechanical engineering conducts a
demonstration in a thermal science class at a doctoral institution.*

The Origins of The Teaching and Learning Project

Seeing is for me a way of knowing, photography a way of thinking. A photograph can embody a complete thought or an entire story; a series of photographs can shape a narrative or make an argument. Words tap the ideas that the visual holds and carry them further.

—*Anne Whiston Spirn (2008, xi)*

What I think I was most pleased with [in the photographs] is how I'm working with students and how they are working with me. This is one of the good days. You can go back to this and say, "this is why I teach."

—*humanities instructor and participant in The Teaching and Learning Project, baccalaureate institution*

Photographs and Higher Education

What Teaching Looks Like: Higher Education through Photographs is not just another book about improving higher education: it is a call to think differently, through and with the visual medium of photographs, about teaching and learning. This book is based on fifteen years of documentary photography work by Martin Springborg under the broad title *The Teaching and Learning Project*, which is the most comprehensive photographic exploration to date of contemporary postsecondary education in the United States. The project has resulted in tens of thousands of images, multiple exhibits and articles (e.g., Springborg 2013; Springborg and Horii 2016; Lang 2018), and insights not only about the state of teaching and learning in US colleges and universities, but also an argument for the ongoing integration of photographs in educational change and improvement efforts in and beyond the United States.

Before we share more about the origins of the project and what to expect in this volume, we invite you to reflect with us on the premise of this work— why photographs? If you have ever taught anything, or learned anything, and it changed you, then you may know how hard it is to explain the process well. Take a moment to consider how you articulate the holistic experience of those moments when the learning or teaching felt important, deep, and impactful— the moments when you were in the midst of changing, but didn't know it yet; the moments before you or your student had any flashes of insight. While you may struggle with precise words for your experience, images can help, though not the kind you have likely encountered of teaching and learning. Authentic photographs, in the traditions of art and documentary photography, are one way to capture and express the richness of these teaching and learning moments. The photographs on the pages that follow invite you in, behind classroom doors and to campuses you might never visit in person. They invite you back, perhaps, to your own memories of moments in which you taught or learned, those moments that changed the course of your life and set you on your current path.

They also offer new perspectives. By pausing to look closely at moments in time in the work of postsecondary teachers and learners, we have the opportunity to notice details and interactions that otherwise pass by too quickly. Photographs give us access to insights beyond what surveys and datasets provide: not only what teaching entails, and how it is changing, but what it means to the people and institutions involved in changing teaching practices. Through traces that we can observe in the images, we can face the history of social and physical structures and challenges embedded in higher education practices. We have the chance to appreciate the emotions, chaos, and hidden forms of labor that are inherent to teaching in colleges and universities, but which have remained largely unseen; once shared through images, we have a better chance of grappling with them openly. Through these affordances, along with the purposeful work of faculty, staff, and administrators, campuses are beginning to employ photographs to support their educational improvement efforts.

This book primarily addresses people working in higher education, especially those dedicated to helping students, faculty, and institutions succeed, and those who think that colleges and universities can and must improve to better serve learners. We focus on teaching, with recognition that teaching involves faculty across appointment types and ranks, as well as students serving as teaching and learning assistants, administrators, and staff, along with academic, educational, and faculty developers. The chapters and accompanying online resources offer people who teach and who support teaching both immediate insights and tools to engage with a wide variety of audiences in newly meaningful ways about their work. The volume and accompanying resources also invite people who are working to improve higher education to reflect and approach change in new ways, whether they are working within colleges and universities or in other kinds of organizations such as foundations, non-governmental organizations, or policy institutes.

As you view the photographs that follow in this introductory chapter, we invite you to pause and reflect on each, asking yourself what you see that is familiar or known, what you see that is new or unexpected, and how these images convey to you what teaching looks like. The short captions that appear with the images briefly identify the people, roles, academic disciplines or settings, and the types of institutions, broadly (we discuss in more detail how we refer to participants in *The Teaching and Learning Project* in captions and quotes later in this introduction). You may also access more detailed descriptive text to use alongside or in place of the photographs and short captions on the book's website at https://www.CenterForEngagedLearning.org/books/what-teaching-looks-like.

0.02
A faculty member in media studies speaks to students in an introduction to media studies class at a doctoral institution.

0.03
*A faculty member in Spanish
conducts a group discussion
with students in a heritage
Spanish speakers' program at
a doctoral institution.*

One of the instructors whose classroom Martin photographed as part of *The Teaching and Learning Project*, a humanities professor at an associate's degree (two-year) college, described their experience of viewing and discussing images from their class this way: "This isn't just about having someone come to a classroom and take photos of you and your students. This isn't just description." Indeed, *The Teaching and Learning Project*, as it positions images and text on equal footing, offers a form of "thick description" (Geertz 1973)—a visceral term for "a rich and layered account that does not result in a 'solution'. . . but can illuminate" a subject (Boys 2011, 7). Here, that subject is higher education and this volume invites you thickly into the remarkable and important endeavors of teaching and learning.

For our exploration to work, we ask you to trust us in a particular way. An anthropologist's perspective on photography helps explain why: "The difference, however difficult to photograph, between a twitch and a wink is vast, as anyone unfortunate enough to have had the first taken for the second knows" (Geertz 1973, 6). Though this book contains images of neither winks nor eye twitches, the larger question of whether these images accurately convey the subject matter of postsecondary teaching and learning is worth addressing.

While we promise to be truthful—to not show you a twitch and call it a wink—you don't have to take our word for it. Throughout the work of *The Teaching and Learning Project*, we have been transparent in our discussions with teachers whose classrooms were photographed about the fact that photographs are themselves acts of interpretation. As participants viewed images of themselves and their students, we made sure to call attention to the subjectivity of the photographs: what Martin chose to include and exclude, which of the many hundreds of images made during a typical class he chose to edit and present, how his perspective could highlight or direct attention away from various facets of the original scene. You will read their reflections on these photographs, and on the authenticity that they capture, throughout the book. Subjectivity here has led to a form of truth.

Our positions as directors of centers for teaching and learning has likely contributed to this effect. As experts in postsecondary teaching, we may perceive certain kinds of educational interactions that others may not notice; we do the same when we observe classes and discuss teaching strategies with colleagues at our institutions. We may focus and linger on nuances that elucidate the difficult-to-articulate aspects of learning that we invited you to reflect on earlier. Though we may show you views of college and university classrooms that you have not encountered before, the interplay between the educational settings, the photographer's experiences, and the authors' knowledge and commitments all contribute to a perspective that is both accurate and novel, while also holding true to the experiences of those portrayed. In other words, "a good interpretation of anything—a poem, a person, a history, a ritual, an institution, a society"—and we would add: a photograph, a classroom, an educational interaction—"takes us into the heart of that of which it is the interpretation" (Geertz 1973, 18). We care deeply about getting to the heart of teaching and learning in higher education, so that colleges and universities can improve what they do and better serve students; photographs offer powerful and as yet underutilized ways to do so.

0.04
Students in an extracurricular tango class at a doctoral institution practice steps with their partners.

0.05
*A student in an African
studies class at a doctoral
institution takes a moment to
read before the instructor and
other students arrive.*

0.06
A graduate teaching assistant works with students during a physics recitation section at a doctoral institution.

0.07
A student takes a break in
a common area at a doctoral
institution.

Origin Stories

This book emerged out of an ongoing collaboration between the authors, both educators, one in fine arts, the other in science, working in institutions ranging from community colleges to research universities. In the chapters that follow, we will often write as co-authors (we) and at times share individual perspectives and experiences (I); when doing the latter, we will identify the writer in a brief parenthetical comment. We have collaborated extensively on all aspects of this volume: Martin made and edited the photographs, while Cassandra contributed to selection and sequencing; Cassandra drafted most of the text, while Martin took the lead on certain sections; both collaboratively planned and edited the entire volume. Here, we discuss our individual origin stories with *The Teaching and Learning Project* to introduce our voices and backgrounds, and then discuss the context of prior work and scholarship involving photographs and education.

Martin

When I first started making the kind of work that would eventually lead to *The Teaching and Learning Project*, it was out of a need to return to a way of working I had become accustomed to as a graduate student—to immerse myself in making, to express curiosity about the process and result at all times, to neglect all else in researching a topic, and to tease it apart until ready to share some profound discoveries with the world. In just a few years of teaching full-time, this part of me had atrophied. I was giving every creative curiosity, every impulse to make art, to my students and their work, which, at the time, is what I believed every faculty member worth their salt should do.

I started talking to my colleagues about it. At my small community college, all faculty participated in graduation ceremonies to show support and congratulations to students. I was in line with my colleagues, at once expressing joy at our students finishing and commiserating about the late nights spent grading their work. I was not the only one who felt they had dropped everything else to teach. Someone mentioned undergraduate research; someone else talked about using their own writing or research as an example in their classes. And I realized in line for that graduation ceremony that I could create a project for my students and me to work on together. It was a perfect solution to creative atrophy.

The early seeds of *The Teaching and Learning Project* were my first entry point into what became a sort of undergraduate research effort in my studio art classes. I presented this project idea to my students as an opportunity to work on a project together, from concept to creation to exhibiting finished pieces. It was to be a 16-week learning exercise in producing documentary work that would speak to both their and my experiences in higher education.

The best time to approach a documentary project on any topic is debatable. There is something to be said for knowledge of the subject you are about to document. There is also something to be said for beginning a documentary project when you are new to the subject, when you haven't yet learned most of what there is to know about it. At this stage, even aspects that experts would consider mundane are exciting, and often remain so because you discovered them yourself. When I started this student-faculty collaboration a little less than three years into my teaching career, I was still learning what it meant to be a faculty member. Most of my students, likewise, were new to being students, having not yet completed their first year of college. Many of them were also first-generation students, the first in their families to go to college. We all set out to photograph what we did not yet fully know, and it was exciting to learn about each other and our relatively new environments and roles through photographs.

The images from that first semester were not as refined as those that I produce today, but they were beautiful in their own imperfect way, and the student work was honest in its imperfections. Every new set of images made for great

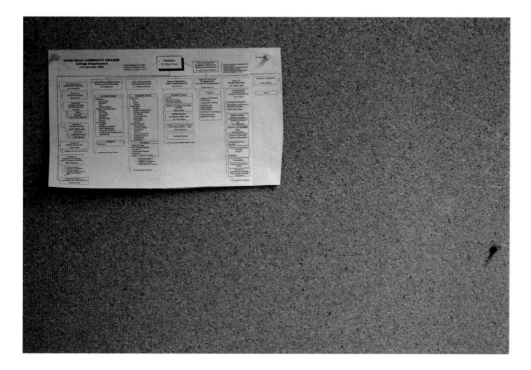

0.08
An organization chart pinned outside a faculty member's office at an associate's institution.

discussion during critique sessions, leading to more questions and more topics to be explored. The photographs made in that class illustrated the many challenges both students and faculty face in postsecondary education today. Student photographs depicted the reality of attending multiple institutions, as well as balancing coursework with employment, home life, and what little remains of social life. Photographs of faculty, likewise, revealed the many duties this role encompasses—including the amount of work and time spent outside of the classroom.

0.09
*Faculty members participate
in an interdisciplinary meeting
at an associate's institution.*

Neither my students nor I had a complete picture of what the other's experience was like, and photographs helped us fill in the gaps. In those early photographs, I reflected on aspects of the work of teaching in postsecondary institutions that defied popular culture ideas of this work and did not fit some of my preconceived notions of what teaching at this level should look like. I was able to show my students, and document for myself, the otherwise invisible non-classroom time that faculty engage in: teachers in their offices, conference rooms, libraries, and hallways, directly engaged with students, faculty colleagues, and administrators, doing work that is necessary for classroom teaching to occur. My students showed me, and revealed to themselves, the unspoken totality of their lives as students, including the barriers they overcame daily to get to class, the ways they juggled studying alongside work and family life (and sleep), and the messy yet beautiful effort they dedicated to their education.

As the project grew, these early themes of revealing hidden work, acknowledging the depth of what it takes to teach and learn in today's colleges and universities, breaking down divisions, and fostering greater connection and collaboration carried through to other campuses I visited, as well as beyond campus borders and into student and faculty work in their surrounding communities.

0.10
A faculty member exchanges materials in his office between classes at a baccalaureate institution.

0.11
A faculty member works in a classroom between class sessions at an associate's institution.

0.12
An advisor for international students works at her desk between meetings at a baccalaureate institution.

0.13
A faculty member and dean from an associate's institution meet at a local diner.

0.14
A faculty member and student discuss projects during an architectural design studio critique session at a doctoral institution.

Cassandra

I first encountered Martin's photographs in 2011; he shared some of his early photographs from *The Teaching and Learning Project* while we worked together on organizing the annual conference for the Professional and Organizational Development (POD) Network in Higher Education. I was immediately struck by the reality, relevance, and powerful visual insights into the nuances of teaching and learning that I noticed in his photographs. I had never seen anything like them. At the time, I had been involved in faculty development and educational improvement efforts at two different institutions for about a decade. As I still am today, I was deeply committed to a career path focused on improving teaching and learning, especially in the sciences but also across academic disciplines, with a focus on equity and inclusion.

My work in centers for teaching and faculty professional development in higher education had afforded me the opportunity to observe teaching and learning in hundreds of classrooms, sometimes as a consultant invited by an instructor seeking feedback, sometimes using video recordings as a basis for consultations on teaching approaches and methods. Even having seen so much, I found that these images offered something that neither my direct experience nor the video recordings did. They captured the moments that mattered—not for their perfection, and not always for their exemplary representations of good teaching, but for what they revealed about the experience of teaching, the subtlety and fleetingness of connections between teachers and students, and the imperfection and evolution of these relationships and processes. They also showed classrooms, faculty, and students as they are today, on actual campuses, rather than an idealized or fantasy version thereof.

I was drawn to the photographs as potential contributors to educational change efforts. In 2012, I had just taken a new job at a different institution and was starting up a brand-new center for teaching and learning on a campus that had not previously offered organized, ongoing faculty development programs. While setting up a website and looking for suitable photographs, I made a revealing discovery. Every institutional image of teaching was a staged stereotype of science education: a lone professor, in front of large chalkboards full of equations, speaking to silent and attentive rows of students taking careful notes. Yet, as I met with faculty, graduate and undergraduate teaching assistants, and students, I knew this was far from the whole story. Yes, some lectures like those in the stereotypical images were happening, but so were other kinds of teaching interactions.

I found myself explaining different kinds of teaching to people in various roles at the university and struggling to convey the possibilities. At other times, I left conversations with the sense that my colleagues and I were not on the same page about the wide range of educational interactions that were already happening. The pervasive image of teaching as instructor, chalkboard, and passive students was getting in the way of reimagining teaching and committing to positive change.

Within the context of early freedoms that come with new endeavors, I approached Martin with a proposed experiment. What if he made photographs that reflected the reality of teaching at my institution today? What if those photographs could expand the visual lexicon for what teaching and learning means to the institution and community? What if we could show, rather than just tell, what teaching looks like?

Martin agreed to visit and make photographs at Caltech, the first institution outside of Minnesota to become part of *The Teaching and Learning Project*. Both Martin's visit and the photographs that he made opened up new conversations with faculty. They also allowed me to convincingly share the wide range of teaching and learning approaches already underway. The project reflected back to my community their as-yet-unspoken commitments to student learning. I saw these commitments in the intensity, thoughtfulness, and meaning captured in moments of teaching and learning in our lecture halls, seminar rooms, and teaching labs. Others saw it too, and this helped the institution tell its teaching story through its publications. It let the walls of the new teaching center, from its very early days, reflect the actual teaching context, and for faculty and student visitors to see themselves in the space. This intervention was one factor in the rapid growth in services, deep engagement with the university community, and positive impacts that the center has enjoyed (reports on the work of the Caltech Center for Teaching, Learning, and Outreach are available at http://ctlo.caltech.edu).

Based on the Caltech visit in early 2013, Martin and I wondered what would happen if we began to bring photographs into consultations and discussions about teaching in new ways, which led to the development of a consultation process, protocol, and formal research study (Springborg and Horii 2016). In the years since, we have continued to develop and explore the role of photographs in campus change processes together, at Caltech and at other institutions.

0.15
*A lecture hall sits empty
prior to class at a doctoral
institution.*

0.16
A faculty member in history facilitates a class discussion during a European history class at a doctoral institution.

0.17
A faculty member in mathematics facilitates small group discussions during a large mathematics class at a doctoral institution.

0.18
A faculty member in statistics speaks to students in an introduction to statistics course at a doctoral institution.

Prior Work: Photographs and Education

To be sure, others have photographed in educational settings prior to this effort. In the 1940s and 1950s, for example, *Look Magazine* published university profiles in the form of photographic essays, including several by Stanley Kubrick; these pieces tended to highlight sports, undergraduate student life, and other facets of university existence, relying on thematic tropes and often-staged images in line with the popular photo magazine's interests in telling captivating stories about modern life (Mather 2013). Several decades later, in *American Classrooms*, Catherine Wagner focused on the physical stuff and spaces of all kinds of classrooms of the 1980s, from preschool to beauty school, language labs to science labs, and everything in between—always without people (Tucker 1988). With yet a different approach, Dawoud Bey, in his *Class Pictures* project, created striking photographic portraits of high school students and exhibited them with the students' written reflections (Bey 2018). More broadly, various archives contain historical photos of classrooms (e.g., Caltech Archives 2017 and 2021), online collections have documented particular aspects of college and university spaces through photographs (Bruff 2018, Cruz et al. 2021; note that the latter work is also based on Martin Springborg's photographs), and institutional marketing photos abound. But there is little else in the way of substantial bodies of serious photographic work focusing on US education at the postsecondary level.

Wagner and Bey's projects represent a useful dichotomy for anticipating what you will find in this book and how to approach your engagement with it. Wagner built on the premise that classrooms "have been reasonably unerring reflections of the broader culture that has encompassed them from the outside. . . . The physical artifacts themselves . . . are mirrors of the day and the mood" (Morris 1988, 8); based on this premise, Wagner's photographs did not require teachers or students. Bey, in contrast, not only portrayed students, but also collaborated with them, with their schools, and with the museums and galleries that would ultimately exhibit the work—a process that "literally changed institutions and the professional orientation of practitioners" (Terrassa 2018, 194). Martin's images capture and call for attention to physical spaces and things, but they are also bursting with the people who teach and learn in those spaces. *The Teaching and Learning Project* seeks not to mirror the culture, but to enhance our common understanding of the value, shortcomings, and potential of higher education, and ultimately to help transform it for the better, in collaboration with institutions, educators, staff, and students.

With the presence and interactions of the people involved in higher education so central here, we will also at times reflect on academic identities. Anna Hunter's explorations of "snapshots of selfhood" explored the "use of photography as a medium through which to present, represent, and interpret" academic work and professional identity, in her case through visual autoethnography using a small number of images from and about her work life (Hunter 2020, 310). With a much wider and more diverse set of photographs in terms of subjects and settings, this volume will often invite you into the process of "exploring lived experience through photographs," using them as "reflexive prompts" (Hunter 313, 314) to spark insight and discovery—a process which our work has explored through discussions with educators whose classes were photographed in *The Teaching and Learning Project* since 2013, resulting in a study documenting the kinds of incidents of reflection prompted by thinking with photographs, including those about their own self concepts and identities (Springborg and Horii 2016). Importantly, we found that photographs often affirmed or had positive impacts on postsecondary educators by demonstrating, in a very different way than they had previously experienced, their accomplishments as teachers, their values and commitments, and their meaningful interactions with students.

In the chapters that follow, reflections prompted by and explored through photographs can affirm, challenge, and help resolve apparent contradictions in academic roles and identities, particularly as they relate to tensions in adopting new teaching practices and perspectives, messiness and chaos in teaching and learning, and change agency. Despite contradictions and messiness, the images in this volume, from a wide array of postsecondary campuses across the United States, also reveal a pattern of shared responsibility and passion for educating our next generation of thinkers, innovators, artists, and scientists. This collaboration is visible in photographs from rural and urban technical and community colleges, large state systems, public land grant institutions, research institutions, and private liberal arts colleges. It is visible in photographs made during department meetings, in faculty shared governance, in classrooms at introductory and advanced levels, in open forums, and in faculty-administrator breakfast meetings at local diners. So prevalent is this theme that when campus communities reflect on their work through these photographs, they are often moved to discuss ways they could recognize the exceptional efforts of their colleagues and work even more collaboratively. It is vital for those whose work is concentrated within one area of a college or university to see, understand, and empathize with their colleagues from other campus sectors.

Distinct from prior work, that is the ultimate intent of this project and book—to make the work of higher education visible, especially to readers engaged in it, fueling deeper understanding, motivation, and methods to effect positive change. Secondarily, postsecondary educators may find ways to leverage the resources in and accompanying this volume when engaging with external stakeholders, policymakers, and the public, as these photographs challenge the sometimes antiquated images and stereotypes of higher education and educators (e.g., Levy 2012; Sturdevant 2020; Hunt, Blethen, and Stewart 2019). In order support your engagement with these materials and meet these goals, the next section offers guidance on reading both photographs and text together, drawing upon our work with faculty, staff, administrators, and students.

What Do You See? A Guide to Looking and Reading

You may not have encountered a book like this before, particularly one with the photographs and the discussion positioned as "coequal . . . and fully collaborative," as they are here (Agee and Evans 1960, xv). This relationship between text and image means that the writing will not tell you exactly what to think about each photograph, but will instead spark your thinking and inform your awareness of your own observations of the photographs. The photographs will not illustrate exactly what is discussed, either, but they frequently inform or extend the discussion in the text. As a reader, you may find it productive to give equal attention to the text and the photographs; we suggest that you try to generate a similar amount of thought, reaction, and annotation, whether a section contains text, photographs, or both.

We recognize that photographs are an inherently visual medium, and therefore are not equally accessible to all readers. In order to make the full volume as accessible as possible, more detailed descriptive text is available for each image. The descriptive text goes beyond the brief context provided in the captions to narrate the main subjects and actions in each image, note prevalent traits of the people, locations, and settings, and share information about the composition, framing, and qualities of light in the image. Our approach to these descriptions is based on guidance from the Web Accessibility Initiative, the Diagram Center, and Cooper Hewitt; the Cooper Hewitt Guidelines for Image Description, in particular, are used by the Smithsonian Design Museum for its image descriptions. You may access the descriptive text in the online resources on the book's website at https://www.CenterForEngagedLearning.org/books/what-teaching-looks-like.

The reflective questions below may equally be applied to your engagement with descriptive text as to the images themselves.

We invite you to attend to the images in this book with a simple question, one that we asked many of the instructors you'll see in these photographs: What do you see? Other fruitful reflections can follow from that one simple inquiry:

- What stands out to you when you look closely at the photographs?
- Is there anything surprising in the images? If so, why and how do the images run counter to your expectations?
- What do you feel and think in response to your observations?
- How novel or familiar are these feelings and thoughts, and why do you think that might be the case?
- What is missing from the photographs and why might that be so?
- What do you think could be beyond the borders or frame of the photograph, and why might that be important to consider?
- What other questions about the classroom, setting, teacher, students, or other aspects of the scene come to mind?
- How do your observations affect your understanding of teaching, learning, and higher education?
- What do the images prompt you to want to recognize, investigate, celebrate, or change?

Each chapter will begin with an opening image, typically chosen for the particularly powerful visual statements it makes about the chapter's themes. You may wish to pause and make your own observations about that image, on its own or together with the chapter epigraphs, before going further. At times, the text will introduce specific questions about a photograph or a series of images; these prompts offer additional ways to deepen your visual reading and reflection. Each chapter will end with a series of additional questions for further reflection. Throughout the book, as you alternate between reading text and examining photographs, allow your reflections on each to be informed by the other, and keep coming back to the fundamental question in your looking: What do you see? You can begin with the photographs in this chapter, which showcase a wide range of institutional settings, disciplines, and details worth seeing.

You may be surprised to find that for both image captions and quotes from instructors who participated in *The Teaching and Learning Project*, we do not identify the people or institutions by name. Instead, we refer to the categories of colleges or universities using the 2018 Carnegie basic classification categories for US institutions (Carnegie 2018): associate's institutions, which grant two-year undergraduate degrees; baccalaureate institutions, which grant four-year undergraduate, or bachelor's, degrees; master's institutions, which grant graduate-level master's degrees in addition to undergraduate degrees; and doctoral institutions, which grant doctoral degrees in addition to those mentioned above. We also mention the broad disciplinary field, such as science, technology, engineering, and mathematics (STEM), humanities, technical/professional, or social sciences, and for those with different roles or multi-department appointments, do not specify the field. The instructors who were photographed and interviewed included tenured, pre-tenure, and non-tenure track faculty; we also do not specify the nature of their instructional appointments in captions and quotation attributions.

This approach aligns with the research conditions under which data from participants' interviews were recorded; this research design encouraged candid sharing by assuring that participants' words would not be associated with specific photographs. However, our identification scheme also serves the following purposes. By removing cues about institutional status and reputation, as well as names and types of faculty appointments, we invite you to encounter each image and each instructor's perspective at face value, without as many expectations about the conditions, funding status, public or private context, or other assumptions as might be present with more specific identification. Indeed, each of the Carnegie classifications highlights consistency in the kinds of degrees offered, while also including diverse institutional characteristics in other dimensions, such as enrollment numbers, demographics, and specific academic disciplines and professional fields of emphasis. We have often found that the approach prompts readers to focus on deeper, more salient aspects of teaching and learning interactions, especially in the photographs, and to locate unexpected commonalities across contexts (e.g., the presence of lecture halls that appear quite traditional or flexible classrooms that facilitate extensive student engagement, across disciplines and institutional categories). As you look, you might also consider what information you have, and what information you wish you had, for each image and participant reflection, and what difference you find it makes in your interpretation and thought process.

You may have already noticed that the photographs are all presented in black and white, rather than full color. When using these photographs in teaching consultations and showing them in broader college and university settings, we've found that the absence of color in the photographs helps viewers focus more clearly on the teaching and learning interactions. For example, one instructor, after seeing both color and black and white versions of the photographs from her class, noted that a brightly colored piece of clothing pulled her attention in the color photos, to the extent that she only noticed interactions that were more relevant and helpful for her reflections on teaching when looking at the black and white photographs. While color images have many good uses, we hope that the black and white format will support your reflections and insights in conjunction with the images presented here.

We will draw you into reflecting on the photographs through thematic chapters focusing on classroom interactions, student perspectives and the role of emotion, the productive chaos of teaching and learning, the physical and technological environment, learning beyond campus borders, the hidden work underlying higher education, and the process of postsecondary educational change through photographs. Throughout the book, we will draw on the literature of both higher education and photography for context and frameworks to help us reflect through and with photographs. We will also point out relevant supplementary resources and guides, including expanded discussion questions, close reading examples of particular images and sets of images, guides for making photographs and hosting exhibits at your institution, and sample guides to consultations, conversations, and workshops based on photographs representing teaching in higher education, available at https://www.CenterForEngagedLearning.org/books/ what-teaching-looks-like. As part of the Center for Engaged Learning Open Access Book Series, the book itself is published under a Creative Commons license that allows you to share unmodified material with attribution and for non-commercial purposes; more information about this Creative Commons license is available at https://CreativeCommons.org/licenses/by-nc-nd/4.0. Whether you teach at a postsecondary institution, work in a center for teaching and learning, serve as an academic staff member or administrator, or enroll as a student, your reflections are important. We hope that you find many opportunities for discussion and change.

0.19
*Students work from a live
model during a drawing
course at an associate's
institution.*

0.20
Students practice during a tuba and euphonium class at a doctoral institution.

0.21
A student grabs a snack between taking notes during a large mathematics class at a doctoral institution.

0.22
A faculty member in operations and information technology management at a doctoral institution asks questions during an otherwise student-led class session.

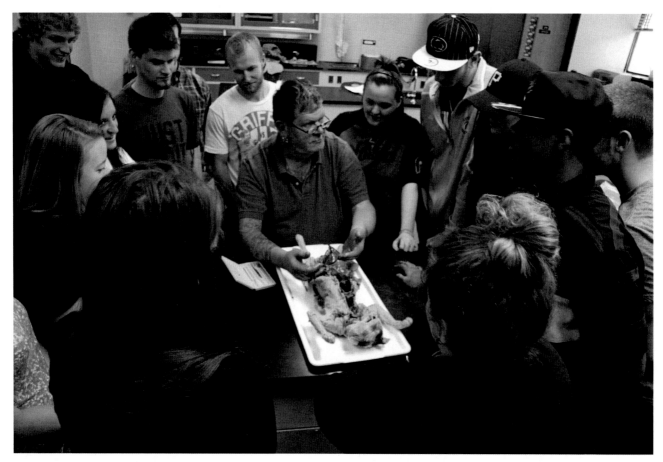

1.01
*A faculty member in biology performs a dissection for students
in an anatomy and physiology class at a mixed baccalaureate/
associate's institution.*

CHAPTER 1

Classroom Interactions

The Heart of Teaching and Learning

Classroom teaching . . . is perhaps the most complex, most challenging, and most demanding, subtle, nuanced, and frightening activity that our species has ever invented.

—*Lee Shulman (2004, 504)*

If I were lying on my death bed, I would want to look at these pictures to know that I did some good teaching.

—*humanities instructor and participant in The Teaching and Learning Project, baccalaureate institution*

Toward a Shared Picture

Imagine this scenario, which describes the experience of one-third to one-half of incoming first-year college students in the early part of the 21st century in the United States: you are the first in your family to attend college and tomorrow is the first day of classes (NCES 2019b). You have skimmed the college's website and maybe you have been to campus for a tour and some orientation sessions. None of those visits included a real class. What do you expect your classes to be like? What picture is in your mind's eye?

It is likely that your image of a college classroom has been shaped by website and brochure photos, which are often staged or edited to portray an idealized archetype of a college experience (Willers 2019), or perhaps by iconic film scenes, more often than not involving a professor, a chalkboard, and mostly bored or passive students. But none of these visual narratives scratch the surface of today's postsecondary educational experiences.

Why don't we, collectively and publicly, have a more complete and nuanced sense of what actually happens in college classrooms? My work as an educational developer, having founded and directed centers that focus on "helping colleges and universities function effectively as teaching and learning communities" (Felten et al. 2007), gives me a special perspective on this question (first-person statements in this chapter are in reference to Cassandra Volpe Horii). I have observed hundreds of classes, discussed postsecondary educational experiences with students and their instructors in considerable depth, and collaborated on the creation of course materials like in-class activities and interactive digital elements for both in-person and online instruction. Yet until I saw images from *The Teaching and Learning Project* in 2011, at which time I had already spent twenty years in higher education as an undergraduate, graduate student, postdoctoral fellow, fac-

ulty member, administrator, and educational developer, I had never encountered an authentic photograph of a college-level class.

The long wait for meaningful visual representation of the work of colleges and universities still surprises me. After all, most students and instructors now carry a camera at all times, built into their mobile devices, and social media has turned making and sharing images into a near-constant activity. Is there something special about the college classroom that has kept it hidden from the ever-present eyes of digital photography? We think so, and will explain why

1.02
A faculty member in chemistry answers student questions after a chemistry class at a baccalaureate institution.

through the images themselves, with help from scholars of education and photography, and observations from instructors whose classes appear in the images of *The Teaching and Learning Project*. While we are grateful that classrooms have not been trivialized through abundant selfies, opening classrooms by way of images is crucial if higher education is to improve—for the benefit of every student wondering what their first day of college will be like, and ultimately, for the benefit the world in which they live.

As you encounter the next group of photographs, consider whether, and in what ways, they reinforce or counter the images of teaching and learning in postsecondary institutions that you had before arriving, and that students likely bring with them today.

1.03
A graduate student teaching assistant helps students in a chemistry class at a doctoral institution.

1.04
*Students in a modern dance
class take cues from their
instructor, a faculty member in
dance at a doctoral institution.*

1.05
A faculty member in biology shows plant samples during a lecture in biology class at a mixed baccalaureate / associate's institution.

1.06
A faculty member in physics uses a remote control during a general physics class at a doctoral institution.

1.07
Students engage in small group discussion during a comparative literature class at a baccalaureate institution.

College Classrooms and Photography

It is possible, but unlikely, that postsecondary classrooms have evaded photographic documentation because of a collective belief that the work of teaching and learning is too complex and meaningful. In the 1970s, well before photography's digital age, Susan Sontag proposed that taking photographs can be "a way of certifying experience, [and] also a way of refusing it—by limiting experience to a search for the photogenic, by converting experience into an image, a souvenir" (Sontag 1977, 9). Sontag's description is the antithesis of what many college educators hope and aim for in their classes, where deep thinking, grappling with complexity, and fully engaging in an educational experience are often the goals. We would prefer the explanation that classrooms have been infrequently photographed so as not "to interfere with, to invade, or to ignore whatever is going on" (Sontag 1977, 11) because the meaningful acts of teaching and learning going on there are too important to disturb or diminish.

Unfortunately, persistent undervaluing of the work of teaching offers a more realistic explanation for the scarcity of postsecondary classroom images. Higher education likes hierarchy, whether related to disciplinary status, educational work, or race; as Lindsey Malcom-Piqueux describes the origin of these systems in the US, "socially-constructed racial hierarchies, and the distribution of rights and opportunity on the basis of these hierarchies, were an organizing principle for American society including the higher education system" (2020, 3). While seventeenth and eighteenth century colonial colleges in the US focused on ethical and intellectual questions and drew upon Greek and Latin works to support their own "rationales for human hierarchy" (Kendi 2016, 17), the colonially-minded American projects of agricultural and industrial expansion became a priority for mid-nineteenth century institutions, also fraught with inequities and purposeful exclusion (Boyer 1990; Malcom-Piqueux 2020), and access to leading research institutions in the US continues to be stratified by race and income to this day (Carnevale and Strohl 2013; Tough 2021, 19). Globally, the rise of neoliberal capitalism since the late 1970s has continued to reinforce stratification and inequity in higher education, driven by "near-global . . . competitive markets in public services such as education" (Kumar and Hill 2009, 1).

Such hierarchies affect access to education and the value of different forms of work within higher education. The top of the academic hierarchy tends to emphasize research, or as Ernest Boyer called it, the "Scholarship of Discovery" (Boyer 1990), rather than teaching. Ellen Condliffe Lagemann offers further insight into the lack of respect for the education part of higher education: "It is hardly a secret that people who study and practice education are engaged in low-status work. . . . In various ways, low status has undermined possibilities for developing a strong professional community and generative scholarly traditions" (Lagemann 2002, xii). Lagemann traced the low status of systematic educational study to gendered conceptions of work: "Associated with teaching, which came to be seen as 'women's work' relatively early in the nineteenth century, the very term educational research seemed to be an oxymoron to many notable university leaders" (Lagemann 2002, 232). In the US, institutions most focused on teaching are also disproportionately where racially minoritized students attend college (Carnevale and Strohl 2013; Astin 2016). The continued low status of teaching is further reflected in poorly developed systems for evaluating teaching effectiveness in higher education—something that those seeking to elevate its status are working to change (Weaver et al. 2020). Given these multiple contributors to and indicators of the low status of teaching, it is no wonder that we have had few systematic representations, including visual representations, of what happens in postsecondary classrooms.

Since the early 1990s, advocates like Boyer have advanced the vision of a more balanced and intentional valuing of teaching alongside research and other scholarly activities (Boyer 1990). But without ways to share the work of teaching, creating a professional community has remained challenging. Also in the 1990s, Lee Shulman helped redefine what such community could be and do for teaching: "I now believe that the reason teaching is not more valued in the academy is because the way we treat teaching removes it from the community of scholars. . . . We celebrate those aspects of our lives and work that can become . . . 'community property.' And if we wish to see greater recognition and reward attached to teaching, we must change the status of teaching from private to community property" (1993, 6). Since then, movements such as the Scholarship of Teaching and Learning (SoTL) and Discipline-Based Educational Research (DBER) have emerged, allowing college and university educators to publish and discuss the work of teaching (Hutchings, Huber, and Ciccone 2011; Henderson et al. 2017). High-quality, authentic photographs are another powerful way to collectively share and value the work of teaching and learning in college classrooms, not only within the higher education community, but also with families, neighbors, taxpayers, policymakers, and other public stakeholders.

The early 2020s represent a particularly important time for the higher education community to reflect on how their work is portrayed within and outside of the academy, though top concerns are continuations of ongoing issues. Despite the well-documented potential for college-level educational attainment to contribute to lifetime fulfilment, civic engagement, and earnings, public funding for education in the US has declined precipitously in recent years (Trostel 2015; Tamborini, Kim, and Sakamoto 2015; Whitford 2020)—a trend mirrored globally by the "definitive retreat of the state as a provider of education" (Kumar and Hill 2009, 1). At the same time, colleges and universities have increasingly been held accountable for deficits in student learning and graduation rates, with teaching quality directly implicated in their shortcomings (Arum and Roksa 2011; Bok 2017). We find ourselves in a transition period when it is clear that

1.08
A faculty member in communications opens a public speaking class at an associate's institution with a relaxation exercise.

teaching should be better, but efforts to improve it remain largely unrewarded, with Lagemann's early millennial observation still ringing true: "In recent years, there has been wide complaint about poor teaching, and there have been efforts to place teaching on a par with research in assessing professorial achievement. . . . The status and affective maps of universities have discouraged interest in pedagogy among noneducationists and encouraged the priority they have placed on research over teaching" (Lagemann 2002, xv). While accreditation standards for US colleges and universities do encourage institutional leaders to pay greater attention to teaching now than they did several decades ago and initiatives are underway to incorporate teaching effectiveness into review, promotion, and tenure decisions for faculty, accompanying culture change has remained slow (NASEM 2020). It seems to require more than reports and meetings to make change happen.

Photographs give us a direct line and a visceral way of communicating that the work of postsecondary teaching already contains models and examples with the potential to achieve the changes that colleges and universities are called upon to make. They provide powerful visual evidence of collaborative, authentic learning across disciplines and institutions, while also shining a light on the shortcomings and challenges; this form of documentation and communication has an important role to play in efforts to improve higher education.

1.09
*A faculty member in statistics
conducts a lecture in an
introduction to statistics course
at a doctoral institution.*

1.10

Faculty and graduate teaching assistants in biology hold a meeting about teaching an introductory biology course at a doctoral institution. (Composite image of three photographs made in close sequence.) View a larger version of this photograph on the book website.

1.11

Students participate in a hospitality management class at a doctoral institution. View a larger version of this photograph on the book website.

Educators Encountering Their Classrooms

Shulman conjectured that "if teaching is going to be community property it must be made visible through artifacts that capture its richness and complexity. In the absence of such artifacts teaching is a bit like dry ice; it disappears at room temperature" (1993, 6). By artifacts, Shulman probably meant collections of items showcasing what teaching and learning leave behind: documents and texts, written by instructors and students, in the process of making and completing learning tasks like assignments and exams. He may also have been thinking of audio/visual items like slides, portfolios, or video clips. We do not know if Shulman had photographs in mind, but the images from *The Teaching and Learning Project* make teaching visible in ways that capture its richness and complexity—that same complexity that he found made teaching so very "challenging . . . demanding, subtle, nuanced, and frightening" (2004, 504)—a claim he made especially about primary and secondary teaching, but we find to be true, albeit in different ways, of postsecondary teaching. Here, we will explore how photographs accomplish this feat, in part through the reflections of participants in the project who, usually for the first time, encountered their own classrooms through photographs.

We interviewed college and university faculty who participated in *The Teaching and Learning Project*; their reflections offer important insights about the role of photographs in documenting, sharing, and ultimately improving classroom interactions. Each participating instructor agreed to have their classes photographed, as did the individual students appearing in the images. Some volunteered and others were invited by a campus organizer, such as a dean or director of a center for teaching and learning. In the book's online resources, you can find a "Sample Photograph Release Form," as well as "Sample Institutional Visit Schedules." The courses photographed spanned academic departments and disciplines, including professional fields like business, nursing, and education; humanities; social sciences; and science, technology, engineering, and mathematics (STEM). The interviews were part of a formal research project that was reviewed and approved by the board overseeing research with human subjects at one of our institutions.

The instructors participating in the interviews each received a digital album of selected photographs from their class and had a chance to view them before the interview. Our discussions began with the simple question you encountered in the introduction, "what do you see?" along with several follow-up questions and topics. This process and the results of the research are documented in our 2016 article (Springborg and Horii 2016). This book's online resources include "Photography-Based Instructional Consultation Prompts," an interview guide that may be used to structure teaching consultations with instructors that incorporate photographs from their classes.

For some instructors, the act of having anyone visit, much less document and discuss their teaching, was novel, highlighting the sense of isolation and lack of community they normally experience. For example, an instructor in a technical/professional field at a baccalaureate institution commented: "Sometimes I feel private about what I do in the classroom. But in twenty-six years of teaching, only three (including you) have observed my classes." Unlike primary and secondary teachers, college educators do not necessarily receive training or pre-service practice in teaching. Now, through campus-based centers for teaching and learning, STEM education centers, disciplinary programs, and national programs in the US, more pre- and early-career college teachers are being trained for and practicing teaching together (Border 2011; NSEC 2020; Baker et al. 2014; Hill et al. 2019). Outside of the US, organized centers and educational development programs have also been increasing (Wright 2019) and having an increasing impact on teaching (Gibbs and Coffey 2004; Gibbs 2013). Photographs can contribute to the sense of community, reflection, and professional development on teaching by enhancing early-career training efforts and facilitating discussion among later-career faculty, who may not have had those opportunities early on.

Once classroom doors are open to photographs, you might wonder whether and how still images "capture . . . the richness and complexity" of teaching and learning. A STEM instructor at a baccalaureate institution explained: "[Photography] captures moments in time that in the heat of the battle you don't usually pick up on. I've been very interested in looking at these [photographs]—it reinforces some things I'm trying to do; points out other things I'm not noticing . . . raising my awareness about what might be going on." This instructor's sense of the enhanced observational capacity afforded by still images aligns with what Susan Sontag theorized in the 1970s: that "photographs may be more memorable than moving images, because they are a neat slice of time, not a flow"; "the force of a photograph is that it keeps open to scrutiny instants which the normal flow of time immediately replaces" (Sontag 1977, 17, 111).

Whereas Sontag admonished this photographic trait as "insolent," warning that "truths that can be rendered in a dissociated moment, however significant or decisive, have a very narrow relation to the needs of understanding" (Sontag 1977, 112), we have found that educators often understand something new and impactful through photographs of classroom interactions. Some found an externalized, observable trace of the significant efforts they make to foster positive interactions and productive learning environments. For example, a STEM instructor from a baccalaureate institution observed:

> I really enjoyed a lot of the photos that were several in a series, so I could see— flash, flash, flash—a few photos in a row, almost like an animation. Looking at several, speaking with a group of students . . . [I can see] the group dynamic, the interaction with a student— smiling and talking about something, then in the next second, very focused on whatever the question was. That expression [referring

to a particular image] was "keep my mouth shut and listen to the student . . ." Sometimes you have to stop and listen more.

Others found the slice of time left open to examination to be loaded with insight, allowing them to take note of and celebrate individual students' work, learning, and individuality. For example, a STEM instructor at a baccalaureate institution noticed, "My students are also doing their own hand gestures. [In one image], I put my [water] bottle and notes down so I could use BOTH hands. I also got a real kick out of [another image, where] my hand is flat, and on the other side of the room, my student's hand is flat like mine, using the same hand gesture to illustrate points to each other." A humanities instructor at an associate's institution reflected:

> It was really nice to be able to stop and look at a fixed facial expression. When in the middle of teaching, [I'm] reading body language quickly—I don't get to sit there and observe intently. For example, this student is super quiet in class, but does a lot in small groups and online discussion forums. . . . It's nice to see her smile and attentiveness. I don't get to look at [or] engage with her as much directly in class. . . . Some students come to class after working all night as a home health worker or other [jobs]. . . . No matter how interested, they may look tired. [There's] something amazing about students— they have a clear sense of what they want to do.

Besides holding moments open for thought about what happens in the classroom, these insights extend to their experiences beyond the frame.

Shulman noted that in order for teachers to learn from their experience, "the two most obvious requirements—knowing what you did and accurately identifying the consequences of what you did—can be hard to achieve" (Shulman 2004, 322). When employed to help educators encounter their own classrooms, the photographs of *The Teaching and Learning Project* elicited not only moments of accurate perception, but a long enough pause to recognize the contexts, challenges, and circumstances that are inseparable from the learning process. In fact, in our research, we found a high rate of occurrence of what we called incidents of reflection—times when instructors were able to "surface and criticize the tacit understandings that have grown up around the repetitive experiences of a specialized practice" (Schon 1983, 62) as well as to "come to a clearer understanding of what [they] do and who [they] are" (Brookfield 1995, 214). Such reflections are crucial for professional learning and change, and they provide compelling motivation for growth. Perhaps this is, in part, what higher education has been missing.

We also find in the above reflections a great deal of insight, kindness, dedication, and hope. Perhaps you will see that too, in the gestures, intensity, and engagement shown in the photographs of classroom interactions, here and throughout this volume.

1.12
A faculty member in biology prepares students for group work during a population biology class at a doctoral institution.

1.13
A faculty member in Spanish checks in on students as they work during a heritage Spanish speakers' course at a doctoral institution.

1.14
*A student in a writing course
at an associate's institution
engages in one-on-one
discussion with the instructor.*

1.15
*A faculty member in
chemistry explains a concept
to a student during a
thermodynamics class at a
baccalaureate institution.*

1.16
A philosophy faculty member engages students in debate during an ethics class at an associate's institution.

1.17
*Students complete a lab
assignment during a physics
class at a master's institution.*

1.18–1.21
Sequence of four photographs: A faculty member in mathematics provides individual and group instruction during a calculus class at a doctoral institution.

1.22
An economics faculty member meets with a student after an economics class at a doctoral institution.

1.23
A faculty member and writing center director facilitates a discussion during a writing class at a doctoral institution.

1.24
*A faculty member in English
speaks to students during a
comparative literature class at
a baccalaureate institution.*

1.25
Led by a faculty member in art and archaeology, classics, and English, students engage in dramatic reading during a communication and theatre class at a doctoral institution.

1.26
A faculty member in African American studies and English speaks to students during a literature class at a doctoral institution.

Strengths, Shortcomings, and Change

This volume invites you to build a new and more complex mental image of post-secondary teaching, and in doing so, become more intimate with its strengths, aware of its shortcomings, and committed to positive change. As you experience the text and images, we hope that you open up to a different form of thinking through photographs. We also hope that, rather than reproducing dogmatic arguments, this experience gives you a new angle entirely. As Anne Whiston Spirn explained while working with Dorothea Lange's 1930s photographs and field reports, "seeing is for me a way of knowing, photography a way of thinking" (Spirn 2008, xi). Colleges and universities need enhanced forms of knowing, thinking, and communication to build on what is good and address the serious challenges they face.

At this juncture, higher education has major, intertwined problems to solve, from managing sector-wide economic pressures, to making access and graduation rates better and more equitable, to incorporating more effective teaching methods. While our narrative here will not solve them, thinking with and through images can expand our collective capacity to hold onto the multiple truths and scales that postsecondary educators must grapple with in order to do so. As one humanities instructor at an associate's institution mused: "If all photos had that one student asleep, it would look really different. But to leave that student out, that would also not be good, that's real and informative. . . . It would be weird if every student looked completely engaged and attentive in every photo. There are those great moments, like in *Dead Poet's Society*, standing on desks, but it would be inauthentic if all photos showed that." This is exactly where we must begin—seeing the student who is asleep, the faculty member who is making do with limited time and resources, and the staff and administrators who set up the room and scheduled the class. When we do so, photographs can become, as

Sontag put it, "not just a record but an evaluation" (Sontag 1977, 88)—one that reveals the heart of higher education, in all its richness and complexity, in classrooms around the world.

Questions for Further Reflection

- Which of the photographs in this chapter capture the aspects of teaching that you find to be complex, challenging, demanding, subtle, or nuanced?
- What moments in your own teaching do you wish you could freeze and examine more closely through photographs? What do you think you would find in those images?
- If you had access to photographs of your teaching, how could they complement or contribute to the other ways you document and communicate about your work?
- How could you use authentic photographs of teaching and learning—either those in this chapter or images from your own institution—to prompt reflection on and changes in teaching practices more broadly?
- In what way do your institution's existing photographs value or devalue the work of teaching?
- Examining the photographs in this chapter, what do you notice about the work of faculty teaching? About the efforts of students learning? What surprises you?

2.01
Students in an engineering class at a doctoral institution listen as a faculty member in engineering provides guidance on a group assignment.

CHAPTER 2

Student Perspectives

Views from the Back of the Class and Elsewhere

I think this process has been very interesting. When you were [taking photographs in my class], all was fine. When I first saw [the images], I didn't like them; I didn't like looking at myself. But then I shared them with my students and we talked about them together. That opened up my thinking about them. Faculty are not the focal point— it's the whole environment.

—*technical/professional instructor and participant in The Teaching and Learning Project, baccalaureate institution*

What I think I was most pleased with is how I'm working with students and how they are working with me. . . . You can go back to this and say, this is why I teach.

—*humanities instructor and participant in The Teaching and Learning Project, baccalaureate institution*

Close Reading the Classroom

To begin our reflections on student perspectives, consider what you notice in the first image in this chapter. Do you see students working together, collaborating? Does their focus stand out, or does something else catch your attention? Does it seem like a typical moment in today's educational settings, or something special? Do you see the professor in the foreground, paper in hand, gesturing to the students' work on their shared screen? While the group in the foreground seems immersed, with each student expressing their own version of pensive reflection and cognitive work, you might also become aware of another group in the background, similarly immersed, their body language echoing that of the first group. If only the photograph didn't end there, with light streaming through the windows, you might envision even more such groups, or begin to feel surrounded by them in all directions.

In a sense, there is nothing transcendent here: no apparent insight or a-ha moment. No one seems especially entertained. This is not a moment of levity or overt happiness. Yet, the guts of teaching and learning today play out through myriad instances like this: students with instructors, students with students, learning and teaching, struggling, thinking, and growing. For every a-ha moment of big, obvious learning, research tells us there are very likely many more moments of deliberate practice, challenging tasks, and effort to make sense of new ideas (Ambrose et al. 2010). If a photograph "isolates, preserves and presents a moment taken from a continuum" (Berger 2013, 20) then moments like these are worth pausing to notice.

What is it like to be a student in today's postsecondary classrooms? How can educators better understand and share students' experiences? Perhaps surprisingly, a skilled photographer in a classroom quickly fades into the background, their movements and actions barely noticed after a few minutes. The camera's lens,

2.02
A student in a math class at a doctoral institution raises a hand for assistance.

then, has the unique ability to access all corners and perspectives in a classroom, and through these photographic perspectives, present a new view of today's classrooms and learning environments, in which learning is nuanced, rich with meaning, and of pressing importance.

Toward Learner-Centered Education

The idea of a paradigm shift holds a special allure in academic communities, so when an article entitled "From Teaching to Learning—A New Paradigm for Undergraduate Education" appeared in 1995, it seemed like we might be onto something big (Barr and Tagg 1995). The authors described a seismic shift already underway, already "lived in our hearts" (those of postsecondary teachers), but in need of clearer articulation. This big shift was to be from an "instruction paradigm," in which colleges' and universities' missions and implicit beliefs put teaching at the center of the action (and all that goes along with a model where transferring or delivering knowledge is the goal: courses, content, credits), to a "learning paradigm," in which the goal is to foster learning by creating environments where students discover and create knowledge (and therefore a focus on the design of conditions in which learners are empowered to succeed). In the years since 1995, the instructional paradigm has also come to be referred to as teacher-centered instruction, and the learning paradigm as student-centered, or more broadly, learner-centered instruction.

Shifting from a teacher-centered to a learner-centered framework also means upending non-trivial expectations and structures, including power dynamics in the classroom, the roles of teachers and students, and the function of content (Weimar 2002). These shifts build on constructivism and liberation pedagogy, philosophies of education in which learning is understood as an active process of constructing new understanding and as a pathway to individual and societal freedom from oppression (e.g., Piaget 1971; Vygotsky 1978; Freire 1993). More recently, educational researchers have produced a slew of evidence showing time and time again that learner-centered approaches—ones that actively engage students in structured, guided activity, situating learning with the student—produce more effective, enduring, and inclusive learning. As these studies have accumulated, meta-analyses and consensus studies have further demonstrated and synthesized the effects of learner-centered instruction at larger scales (e.g., Freeman et al. 2014; Theobald et al. 2020; NRC 2015; NASEM 2016). Advocates for student-faculty partnerships, in which students and instructors work together to design courses, improve their shared learning and teaching experiences, and change educational practices in departments and institutions, point to potentially transformative benefits to this further extension of learner-centeredness (Cook-Sather, Bovill, and Felten 2014). Now, in addition to its place in higher education as a philosophy and a paradigm, learner-centered instruction represents an array of evidence-based methods with the potential to make higher education more equitable for more students.

Higher education still struggles to fully and routinely embody learner-centered instruction. On the bright side, national surveys of US faculty show that learner-centered strategies like class discussions, cooperative learning, and student-selected topics have been on the rise since the 1980s. At the same time, though, the decidedly teacher-centered approach of extensive lecturing has become only slightly less common; in recent years, over half of all US faculty respondents reported using extensive lecturing in all or most of their classes (Stoltzenberg et al. 2019; Eagan et al. 2014). In some disciplines, such as STEM fields, the frequent use of teacher-centered approaches is even higher, and the aggregate numbers also mask differences in teaching methods across faculty demographics, with, for example, women tending to implement more learner-centered approaches than men (Hurtado et al. 2012). Notably, women remain un-

Students in a biology class at a doctoral institution listen and take notes during a lecture.

derrepresented in tenured faculty positions in the US (Hussar et al. 2020, 151) and in higher education leadership around the world (ACE 2021).

Given the complexity and sluggishness of changing the paradigm, it is important that people in higher education show and highlight learner-centered classrooms, making them a central part of the shared narrative among educators, students, and the public. Experts on how educational practices change have argued that symbols—the "cultural artifacts, language, knowledge, myths, values, and vision" and "underlying ways of thinking that give meaning to the structures," such as in an academic department or a postsecondary institution—are crucial elements when culture and practice are changing (Reinholz and Apkarian 2018). In the ongoing process of change from teacher- to learner-centered instruction, photographs should play a more central role. As John Berger, British art critic and novelist known for the book and 1970s BBC series *Ways of Seeing* mused, "Cameras are boxes for transporting appearances" (Berger 2013, 66). The appearances we choose to transport—and what roles, relationships, activity, and content they show—become part of our collective symbols for teaching and learning in college classrooms. If we more often see images showing college teachers as the "sage on the stage" rather than the "guide on the side" (King 1993) even as national data indicate that is becoming less likely, perhaps it is an indicator that our symbols have some catching up to do.

Photographs from the classrooms visited throughout *The Teaching and Learning Project* allow us to see and share what learner-centered instruction looks like, such as the group of images in the next section. In such classes, instructors are not bound to the front of the room; they could be anywhere, poised to help, attending to students' progress on tasks designed to engage and challenge. The expectation of professing is undone. With the photograph's viewpoint surrounded by students, it is their attention, rather than their teacher's, that takes center stage. In foreground and background alike, students attend to one another. Gestures, gazes, and triangulation between learners and the stuff of learning—the papers and calculators and laptops, books and coffee, pipettes and Erlenmeyer flasks—come together to freeze the frame on elusive instants in the complex process of learning in college. As we come to understand and practice teaching as facilitation and as partnership, the visual representation of postsecondary instructors ready to collaborate—holding back, listening, and helping—needs to command as much respect and admiration as earlier archetypes, and we need images alongside research and exposition to make these modes of interaction part of the collective identity of college educators. Likewise, shifting the image of students in college classrooms from receivers to active contributors is vital: students' interactions with fellow students and with themselves are as important as their relationships with the subject matter and instructors (Quinlan 2016).

2.04
A graduate student instructor assists students in a mathematics lab at a doctoral institution.

2.05
*Students in an African
studies seminar at a doctoral
institution engage in
discussion.*

2.06
A faculty member in art history at a doctoral institution observes as students in her art history class engage in a small group exercise.

2.07
A faculty member in chemistry at a master's institution observes as students in his chemistry recitation session work in small groups.

Emotion and Learning

It is not only what students do, but how they feel, that matters a great deal. The emotions that colleges and universities are willing to show, or not show, telegraph to students important expectations about higher education, learning, and more. You may very well approach the images that follow, 2.08 – 2.15, with your own set of expectations and values. Do you gravitate toward some photographs more than others, based on the apparent enjoyment, pride, or intensity of emotion they capture? Do some of these moments seem more collegiate or more academic than others—more in line with what you expect college to look like? How alike or dissimilar are these images from what you have encountered in university and college brochures, advertisements, and websites? (Note that a set of photographs on the theme of emotion and learning, with prompts for observation and reflection, are included in the online resource "Close Reading and Observation Exercises.")

A deeper examination of emotion in the classroom through images offers another window into students' experiences. Scholars of education have advanced the notion that "students are not only intellectual but also social and emotional beings, and that these dimensions interact with the classroom climate to influence learning" (Ambrose et al. 2010, 156). Much past work on emotion sought and found associations between positive emotions—especially more activating ones like enjoyment, excitement, pride, and hopefulness—and desired outcomes like motivation, achievement, and flow experiences (Pekrun et al. 2007). Moments of obvious joy and success, as shown in some of the photographs in the next group of images, capture times when classroom activity itself seems to elicit enjoyment and spontaneous expressions of delight, perhaps due to a flash of insight. Indeed, educators and students alike hope and long for these moments.

But if we are after more than a passing insight or bit of levity, we need to reframe conceptions of emotion in higher education. Even in comprehensive models of affect in learning environments, researchers admit that "the overall effects of emotions on achievement are inevitably complex" and are linked in loops of "reciprocal causation" with other students, teachers, predictions, experiences, and learning itself (Pekrun et al. 2007, 28). Emotions that are not clearly positive or negative—expressions of confusion, absorption in thought, intensity, or struggling to understand—may actually be important signals of deeper learning: "Transformative learning is often initiated when learners come up against their limitations, go beyond the habitual, experience the unaccustomed, meet, split, or break down, face dilemmas, feel insecure, or must make incalculable decisions. Many examples indicate that irregular courses with obstacles, breaks, problems and challenges encourage emotional intensity and innovation, and in this way also promote transformative learning" (Illeris 2014, 11). So perhaps the student cradling head in hand and the one with the furrowed brow on the following pages bring to light necessary moments of engagement and crucial parts of learning, even if we are not so used to seeing them in the official photographs and representations of postsecondary learning.

Photographs represent and convey vital information about students' emotions, learning, and authentic experiences in today's college and university classrooms. As Berger reflected, "A photograph is already a message about the events it records. . . . At its simplest, the message, decoded, means: I have decided that seeing this is worth recording" (Berger 2013, 18). The images that institutional leaders, communications staff, and faculty choose to use, alongside text and other media, convey to students, their families, and the public how higher education matters and what it entails. It should be worth recording that students in college encounter the kind of good challenge—sometimes called "desirable difficulty" (Bjork 1994)—that leads to long-term retention, deep learning, and new possibilities including jobs, careers, and contributions to their communities that will play out over their lifetimes. It should be worth sharing the message that universities are places where students and their teachers experience "passionate thought" (Neumann 2009)—an exhilarating and downright hard place of meaningful discovery. Students deserve to know that the depth of their thinking and feeling—in the midst of learning, not just after, and including their authentic expressions of curiosity, struggle, and joyful success—are all worth recording.

2.08
A faculty member in biology and forestry celebrates a student success in his soil science class at a mixed baccalaureate/associate's institution.

2.09
*A student expresses happiness
after answering a question in
a business class at a doctoral
institution.*

2.10
Students concentrate during a physics exam at a doctoral institution.

2.11
Students in a disability history class at a doctoral institution review articles as part of a class discussion.

2.12
*A faculty member in
communications connects
with students after class at a
baccalaureate institution.*

2.13
*Students engage in discussion
during a writing class at a
doctoral institution.*

2.14
Students use clickers to respond to questions during a statistics class at a doctoral institution.

2.15
Students share and discuss writing samples during a professional email communications workshop at a doctoral institution.

Views from the Back of the Class

The images explored so far in this chapter have largely provided glimpses of what it is like to be embedded alongside today's students, giving those outside of their institutions and classes a close-up perspective. We have not yet shown much, though, the views from the back of the class—something instructors may rarely have a chance to see. In some cases, all is well at the back of the room; for example, one technical/professional instructor at a baccalaureate institution commented, upon viewing photographs of their class, "I like the images of students taking notes. They show the students are engaged with the material. Especially students in the back of the classroom. I did not see that before." But in other cases, images raise new questions, as this STEM instructor from a baccalaureate institution remarked: "Am I getting excited about the topic because I love it and thinking students are with me, but maybe they are leaning back or not as engaged?"

It may be hard to imagine what it is like to be one among a sea of students in today's universities. We offer such views in the group of photographs that follows. Based on data that institutions make public, the percentage of undergraduate classes with fifty or more students at US universities ranges from as low as 5% to over 30% (Public University Honors 2019). Some instructors manage to make even large lecture halls (a frequently used term for fixed-seat auditoriums and a reminder of their intended use) into active, learner-centered environments. In others, the professor appears as a distant figure on the horizon, along with a chalkboard or projector screen. In these examples, it is easy to empathize with students in the back rows, who may not perceive their presence as vital; whether they slump or sleep, attempt to multitask on other work or social media, attend alertly or lackadaisically has no immediate impact on what happens in the room, even as it may be important for their long-term learning.

A striking number of postsecondary students are employed: in 2018, approximately 27% of US full-time students worked twenty hours or more per week, and that figure was 71% for US students attending college part-time (NCES 2019a, Table 503.40). Given these employment rates, it is impossible to know whether a particular lecture hall nap is a result of a night shift, an all-nighter working on schoolwork, or something more whimsical. Students may also experience less risk in the back of the room; sitting in a circle, for example, can be experienced as a form of increased surveillance and coercion (Brookfield 2019), and the same could be true for being positioned closer to the front of a lecture hall. Given the complexity and many demands on students' time and attention, engaging with students purposefully during class through learner-centered and collaborative approaches, while respecting the variety of demands and experiences that they bring into the room, becomes even more important.

There are deeper implications when a student's presence does not seem to matter in the class. If students can find no evidence that they belong, what are they to conclude? Mica Estrada and colleagues note that for historically marginalized and minoritized students—those whose races and ethnicities have been and continue to be far less prevalent in higher education than in the population at large—their "sense of belonging and connection . . . to their academic community is complex and often obstructed. . . . There are real consequences to being in an academic environment that lacks cues affirming inclusion" (Estrada, Eroy-Reveles, and Matsui 2018). This crisis of belonging is especially acute in STEM subjects, where perhaps not coincidentally, learner-centered teaching methods are less likely to be employed than in other fields of study. The antidotes require not only using more learner-centered methods in classes of all sizes (Theobald et al. 2020), but also persistently communicating "kindness, dignity, and connection" (Estrada, Eroy-Reveles, and Matsui 2018).

When such communication occurs, we must also show it, in STEM fields and all disciplines. Let us show what kindness, belonging, and trust are like in colleges and universities. Let us extend that belonging and trust by sharing the reality and poignancy of what it means to learn in college today, through photographs and otherwise.

2.16
Students sit in rows in a large mathematics class at a doctoral institution.

2.17
Students use laptops during a large economics class at a doctoral institution.

2.18
Students participate in a physics class at a doctoral institution.

2.19
*Students show different levels
of engagement in a women's
studies class at a doctoral
institution.*

2.20
Students prepare to work in small groups during a neurobiology course at a doctoral institution.

2.21
*Students use clickers to
answer questions during a
statistics class at a doctoral
institution.*

2.22
Students participate in a large physics class at a doctoral institution.

2.23
Students take notes during a mechanical engineering class at a baccalaureate institution.

Teaching Beyond the Frame

We began this chapter by asking you one of the opening questions that we asked participants in *The Teaching and Learning Project* when we viewed and discussed photographs of their classes with them. But we are also aware of what photographs leave out—what is outside of the image, the selections presented here, and the project as a whole. As much as photographs fill in crucial information, such as perspectives and perceptions of students and of learning that we might otherwise miss, they remain incomplete.

This limitation emerged in our conversations with participants, too. For example, a humanities instructor at a baccalaureate institution shared this: "I was thinking about how the photos reference what's beyond the frame. That's hard to know. What are people thinking? You don't know—that's the thing about photography. It's almost surreal, the possibilities for what surrounds the image." Yet in that same conversation, details in the photographs opened up important aspects of teaching beyond the frame for our shared reflection and meaning-making: the instructor mentioned objects and examples of students' work in the photographs that connected with their lives and interests, and although he did not know everything about his students, he nevertheless valued and appreciated what they each brought to the classroom and how they changed the space, him, and each other.

Berger distills the quality that allows photographs to be so limited, yet evoke so much: "A photograph quotes from appearances but, in quoting, simplifies them. This simplification can increase their legibility. Everything depends on the quality of the quotation chosen" (Berger 2013, 89). The quality Berger references requires both particularity and generalizability. We learn something new from images showing normally inaccessible settings like college classrooms; we have not seen these before. And we recognize our own victories and struggles;

we consider the students beyond the frame and beyond the campus, including those who have not had access to educational opportunities. In encountering the photographic quotation, we realize there is a larger system in which this snapshot is embedded.

We are hopeful that higher education will continue to make progress on its long transition from teacher-centered to learner-centered instruction with an accelerated pace. As we choose how to convey this change, postsecondary educators will continue to talk and write, and we should also show the change through images so that our collective symbols for postsecondary learning align with what we know, and with what students need, from their colleges and universities.

2.24
Students engage in discussion during a women's studies recitation session at a doctoral institution.

Questions for Further Reflection

- If someone were to take photographs of your classes, do you think they would show a more teacher-centered environment, a more learner-centered environment, an environment based on partnership, or a combination? How would you be able to tell?

- What kinds of emotions do you observe in the photographs in this chapter? How comfortable or uncomfortable are you with seeing those emotions in the images? How about in your classes?

- What reactions, emotions, and thoughts arise when you view the images in this chapter showing views from the back of and within large classes? How do you think these views compare with experiences students and faculty have in large classes at your institution?

- Do your institutional images tend to represent learner-centered, teacher-centered, or partnership-based instruction? Why do you think that is the case, and are there differences depending on the context?

- Outside of this volume, have you found examples of institutional images that show emotions that are not clearly happy or celebratory? What role do expressions of absorption, intensity, and challenge play in your institution's values and representations?

- What questions do these and other images raise about what's beyond the frame—about larger, systemic issues faced by students and faculty in higher education settings?

The Beauty of learning

- What does learning look
  like? (feel like someone
  has written about this...)
" learning is messy
- Don't these pictures
  romanticize teaching &
  learning?" YES! That's
  kind of the point.
- What does it look like
  in diff. places?
    - front of auditorium vs.
      back?
    - study sessions

3.01
A page from Martin's notebook, written while photographing an office hour study session at a doctoral institution.

CHAPTER 3

Productive Chaos

The Messy Nature of Education

It's a little chaotic at the beginning. . . . Students are handing in papers, reports, and picking up . . . cards. . . . A lot of times I can joke around with them. I get to know them. . . . You can tell who is having a good day, who is having a bad day. . . . [There are] many [photos] where you really can't tell what exactly is happening. . . . [I] like the interaction of students, the blurred hand and action."

—*STEM instructor and participant in The Teaching and Learning Project, master's institution*

Paradoxically, photography's tendency to be literal-minded, to render extraordinary things matter-of-factly, plays right into the fantastical.
—*Wendy Ewald (2001, 71)*

Learning Is Messy

While making photographs during an open, multi-section statistics group study session, I had a sudden realization about my maybe-secret purpose in *The Teaching and Learning Project* (first-person statements in this chapter are in reference to Martin Springborg). At that moment, I was enveloped in a fairly chaotic scene: amidst hundreds of students studying for an upcoming statistics exam. Students had no. 2 pencils with teeth marks wedged behind their ears. Papers and calculators were handed—or thrown—across tables. Laptops were propped on end and held in the air for optimal group viewing. It was loud, audibly and visually.

3.02–3.03
Sequence of two photographs: Students in a statistics course at a doctoral institution engage in discussion during an office hour.

To an outsider, I'm sure this room would have appeared to be the antithesis of a model learning environment. But there was learning happening here. In fact, I paused to reflect on the beauty of the learning process I was witnessing. I asked myself what learning looks like, in more than a rhetorical way, jotting the note to myself that appears at the beginning of this chapter. Really, I thought, what are we led to believe learning should look like? When we think of photographs or any other images of teaching and learning, we most likely envision the quiet classrooms, libraries, and other spaces so often repeated in both Western and non-Western media and art (University of Minnesota, n.d.). These old images we've held of teaching and learning, if once the standard, no longer apply. No, I thought, this scene playing out in front of me, this is learning. Learning is messy. Learning is beautiful.

Ira Shor and Paulo Freire, in *A Pedagogy for Liberation*, also arrived at the conclusion that education is inherently an aesthetic experience—"a permanent process of formation" and "necessarily an artistic one" (1987, 118) due to the creativity and holistic perception involved in such deep and personal change. This process also involved, for Shor and Freire, "creative disruption" and asking "students to reperceive their prior understandings and to practice new perceptions as creative learners with the teacher" (116), as well as "inviting students to recreate themselves as listeners and speakers" and "reinventing the visual and verbal aspects of the classroom [as] two ways of addressing the destructive arts of passive education" (117). In essence, they argued for more mess and more beauty in learning.

The choices made in a learning environment impact students' whole-being encounters with learning and their process of becoming themselves, their formation. Together, these choices and processes form an aesthetic experience—one that taps into the hard-to-describe realm of the beautiful, the sublime, the chaotic, the fascinating, the wonderous, and other qualities that are deeply felt and sensed, and are powerful potential sources of meaning-making. But we want to stay close to the images here and not get too philosophical; look up aesthetics and you'll quickly get a sense of where that discussion can go. This chapter explores photographs where the messy and wondrous nature of teaching and learning are especially present, where the aesthetics of what teaching looks like are especially accessible, and what they might mean for our changing understanding of higher education.

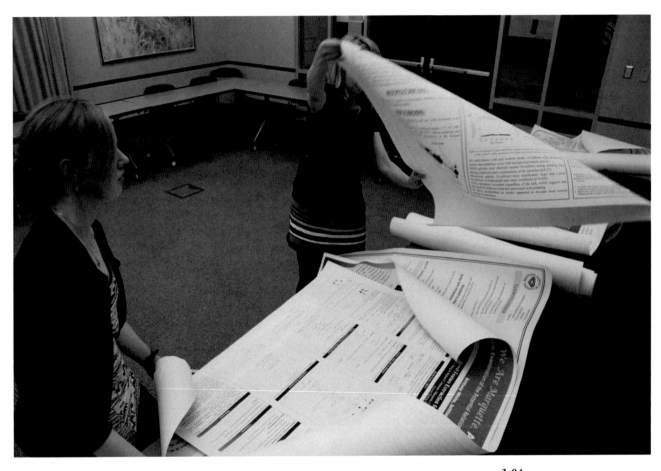

3.04
A writing center director and faculty member in English hangs posters with a student prior to class at a doctoral institution.

3.05
An arts faculty member at a mixed baccalaureate/ associate's institution shuttles supplies during a drawing class.

3.06
A student visits with a faculty member after a comparative literature course at a baccalaureate institution.

3.07
Students at a doctoral institution participate in a guided study group in chemistry.

In the broader collection of photographs in *The Teaching and Learning Project*, it would have been easy to make visual decisions to depict chaotic scenes like the ones here as just that—chaos, as in utter disorder and confusion—and convey to a viewer an environment of anti-learning. Instead, some of my photographs go the other direction and border on romanticizing these kinds of scenes and the learning that takes place within them—an inclination that might make sense. As we've discussed in earlier chapters, the education part of higher education hasn't always been highly regarded, and we are inclined to want to show you what is wonderful about it.

As a photographer, I am certainly not alone in finding a sense of beauty in chaos. I have been inspired by American photographer Emmet Gowin, who found and represented in his photographs beautiful disorder and meaning in subjects from everyday life, in family scenes, in people aging and dying, and in a wide range of emotions and contexts. As Gowin—himself a university faculty member who taught for nearly four decades—put it, "The photograph is able to synthesize what is before the camera in a way that we, ourselves, cannot. The beauty of this synthesis would be the fact that it is a reintroduction to reality. No one view better than another but fresh, something we could never have dreamed up" (Caponigro 1998).

In the end, I have tried with my photographs to neither portray the inherent disorder in teaching and learning as negative, nor idealize it as more appealing than it really is. Rather, I hope to show you what is real and what is beautiful; what is happening and what is possible. One of our participants, a technical/professional instructor at a baccalaureate institution, captured this contradiction well, noting that what stood out in the photographs were the "random things in the classroom that drive me nuts! For example, the cleaning supplies, chairs, printers, the flip paper that has been there forever. I do like teaching in this classroom, however, because it's conducive to interaction. The classroom seems less formal because of some of the chaos or disorganization in the environment."

This discussion, too, walks a fine line between romanticizing and avoiding the chaos, especially when we start talking about the nature of the beauty therein. It's hard to describe a visceral, aesthetic idea in a form other than its original. It's like learning: the layered complexity that emerges through interactions between teachers and students cultivates the kinds of contained, messy challenges that lead to deep growth—where students are secure enough to risk new ways of thinking and being, and pushed enough to need to grow. This process is necessary for civic discourse, understanding and addressing complex phenomena, and engaging in uncomfortable yet productive collaboration. Ultimately, we find beauty in the mess, beauty in portraying the chaos through photographs, and "beautiful risks" (Beghetto 2019) and courage in entering into transformative teaching and learning. Teaching and learning are anything but stifling and serene, and contemporary images of these activities should be just as dynamic as the acts themselves.

It is important in this endeavor to raise up the reality that not everyone finds a positive aesthetic experience in the facets of learning that are messy. Debra Busman, who teaches courses in creative writing and social action at a Hispanic-serving institution with a large population of students from farm-working families, explains: "For these students, as well as for other first-generation students of color and working class white students, told from the jump that they were not *college material*, the very fact of their presence at a university is a charged act of political resistance. . . . [Taking] control of their own narrative . . . can be especially risky for students whose previous success was conditioned upon the very premise of silence and obedience. Many students from working class school districts have been taught that to be a 'good student' meant that you were quiet, well-behaved, that you stayed below the radar" (Busman 2017, 49). For some students, then, participating in less-structured creation and discovery in class can be more a source of danger than learning.

Students take risks to learn. Instructors take risks to teach. Both risk letting go of order and moving into what can seem like a treacherous kind of chaos, all for the sake of remaking themselves. To be frank, I am in awe that learning ever happens, but my experience photographing, and now my ability to show those photographs to you, convinces me otherwise.

To be fair, faculty and students do not always experience such chaos. Kimberly Dark explains: "When I think of teaching, at the college and university levels in particular, the structure of the experience offers safety first. I make a syllabus. We meet at a prescribed time and place and we move through the planned material. . . . We learn by following the examples we've been given, and, at first, the structure of the role *professor* is the life jacket that keeps us afloat. . . . Students do their job and I do mine" (2017, 26-27). Those expected structures are what many of the photographs in this chapter deviate away from. Rather, they may represent what Dark articulates as "favorite moments" in teaching: "when I have a plan, held loosely, a command of the material and a desire to discover more . . . how I just stay present—and risk failing—as I bring that material to students" (29). In recognizing the beautiful messiness of learning, and forgiving when it doesn't work perfectly, the photographs in this chapter may give you the opportunity to explore in new ways your aesthetic understanding of teaching and learning.

Teaching Within Chaos

Similar themes of beautiful, vital chaos emerge when visualizing faculty work; we posit that making sure to include the chaos in visual representations is important for several reasons. The first is clarity about entering the profession of postsecondary teaching. Across the many colleges and universities, and in all manner of institution types photographed for *The Teaching and Learning Project*, the reality of faculty work is rarely neat and orderly. Like real images of student learning, institutions would probably not choose real images of faculty work to advertise to the general public or in faculty recruitment efforts. Yet, faculty work-life depicted in this project is already understood by graduate students entering this job market, hoping themselves to become postsecondary instructors. Either they've embraced it to some extent themselves in graduate teaching assistant roles, or they've witnessed it in their parallel work with their faculty advisors and mentors. In many respects, graduate students are introduced to the realities of faculty work as part of their education—part of the hidden curricula in all graduate programs. That curriculum can be made more transparent with authentic depictions of faculty work.

3.08

Faculty and staff observe as a faculty member in geological and planetary science guides students in an earth sciences class at a doctoral institution. View a larger version of this photograph on the book website.

3.09–3.11
Sequence of three photographs: A faculty member in neuroscience returns graded assignments as students prepare to work in small groups during a neurobiology course at a doctoral institution.

Part of the productive chaos of faculty work comes from the different aspects of what that work entails; the intertwining of those aspects are a key element of the creativity and flexibility that many faculty members experience and that draw them to higher education settings, but it also introduces complexity. Photographs in this project depict the trilogy of faculty work: teaching, service, and scholarship (Kelly 2019). These distinct but related parts of the job are more or less noticeable at some institution types than others, but are nevertheless present everywhere. Teaching includes instruction and extends beyond the classroom to office hours, advising, and other forms of student engagement. Service encompasses faculty commitments to the institution such as committee assignments, leadership roles, and peer review. Scholarship signals the generation of new knowledge; it informs teaching and contributes to broader academic and public conversations through research in one's field, creative work, publications, the scholarship of teaching and learning (SoTL), and other contributions. The lines between these different aspects of faculty work are rarely distinct; they are more like the overlapping bubbles of a Venn diagram, but blurred and fuzzy. Depicting these facets through photographs acknowledges and helps make sense of the importance of all three.

You have been engaging with photographic portrayals of teaching throughout this volume. Here, that work itself may look more disordered. Wiebe et al., in their introduction to an edited volume that brings together postsecondary educators' narratives of how their selves and identities come into play in their teaching, noted that "differences in teaching styles, methods, and philosophies . . . can appear chaotic and messy" (vii). They advise us to "resist the temptation to . . . reduce teaching to tidy boxes and neat platitudes that emphasize only our commonness," and instead to shine light on "our ways of being in teaching, our differences and our commonness [that] come together in a shared sense of humanity" (vii). Wiebe and co-editors sought to illuminate the messiness of teaching through postsecondary educators' stories. Here, we do so through images, which bring a unique power and communicative potential into the complexity of college and university teaching.

Photographs of faculty engaged in important non-instructional aspects of their work also break down popular culture's portrayal of professors and their workdays. The myth is that they spend a couple of hours in contact with their students and the rest of their time thinking deeply in idyllic silence. This popular misconception—that faculty only teach, and do so in not that many hours of the day or week—sometimes makes it difficult for those working within higher education to communicate with those who work in other sectors, to answer questions from, say, legislators who make decisions about higher education funding. Questions, like "why can't you just tell faculty what to do?" miss the deep sense of care among faculty and administrators alike, and those asking these questions seem ignorant of the gravity of responsibility through collaborative governance and the value of faculty scholarship as part of academics' identity and life's work. The photographs of *The Teaching and Learning Project* help illuminate these rarely seen aspects of faculty work, chaotic as these may sometimes be. And in that illumination, they give us a more honest portrayal of higher education—one that may help introduce the work of postsecondary faculty, along with its relevance, to the public conversation.

3.12
A faculty member in biostatistics facilitates a class discussion at a doctoral institution.

3.13
Students retrieve graded assignments after a physics class at a doctoral institution.

3.14
A faculty member in dance leads students in a modern dance class at a doctoral institution.

3.15
*Students stretch during a
modern dance class at a
doctoral institution.*

3.16
Students compare work during a mathematics lab at a doctoral institution.

3.17
Students engage in discussion during a statistics office hour at a doctoral institution.

3.18
Specimens in a geology classroom at a doctoral institution.

3.19
*Multiple overlapping
exposures show students
working in teams during
an earth sciences class at a
doctoral institution.*

3.20
A student solves problems on a dry-erase wall in a writing center at a doctoral institution.

3.21

*A faculty member in
chemistry references notes
during a chemistry class at a
doctoral institution.*

3.22
Students present work in a photography class at a doctoral institution.

3.23
A faculty member in kinesiology guides students in a martial arts class at a baccalaureate institution.

3.24
Students analyze plant samples during a population biology class at a doctoral institution.

3.25
*Students work during a
chemical engineering lab at a
doctoral institution.*

Questions for Further Reflection

- What are your beliefs about how orderly or messy teaching and learning should be? How do you think those beliefs might influence your approach to teaching?
- To what extent do the images that portray teaching and learning in your institution embrace or hide any of the untidy aspects of teaching? In what ways are these representations helpful or unhelpful?
- When might instructors and students need more order and organization and when might exploring some degree of chaos or disorder be helpful? Why?
- What aspects of teaching do you consider to be beautiful? What might the benefits be for instructors and institutions if there were greater recognition of the ways in which teaching and learning can be exquisite?

4.01

Students watch a video in a medical ethics class at an associate's institution.

CHAPTER 4

The Physical and Technological Environment

The Where and How of Teaching

The classroom, with all its limitations, remains a location of possibility.
—*bell hooks (1994, 207)*

Learning activities are always about more than the space; and space
is always about more than just the learning activities that go on in it.
  —*Jos Boys (2011, 85)*

Compromises and Collisions

In higher education, few topics will start a heated discussion as quickly as parking, space, and technology. Parking is beyond our scope, but space and technology figure prominently in the photographs of *The Teaching and Learning Project*. While US higher education headlines over the past decade highlight large private donations and the new buildings, classrooms, labs, and technologies they have made possible, Martin rarely photographed in brand-new spaces. He did not set out to avoid them; they simply weren't dominant in the project's sampling of classes, meetings, and events. The contrast between shiny new campus spaces—prominent in press coverage, fundraising, and admissions materials—and the long-deferred maintenance, much-needed upgrades, and hodgepodge nature of behind-the-scenes classrooms and offices (Marcus 2016) is reflected in the photographs.

Despite these contrasts between new and old, the message in the images is predominantly not one of limitation and decline. Rather, I come away with appreciation for the complex interplay between spaces, technologies, and the people who teach and learn with and within them (first-person statements in this chapter are in reference to Cassandra Volpe Horii). The choices that instructors and students make together to challenge apparent constraints and create the kinds of environments and interactions that foster deep learning and collaboration are particularly compelling.

Higher education, though, can get a little stuck thinking that outdated spaces and technologies mean nothing has changed. A particular mid-fourteenth-century illustration that has been included in many lectures, blogs, theses, and publications on the state of modern education is a ready example (e.g., Pinkerton 2016; Vikberg 2012; Bates 2019). Apart from the robes, hats, parchment, and quills, the illustration has become an icon of sorts because of its familiarity: in it, a professor speaks from a podium to university students in the tiered rows of a lecture hall; some pay rapt attention, while others appear to have dozed off, become distracted by personal technology (their parchments and quills), or started chatting with one another. The illustration is often used to make the point that higher education is painfully slow to change.

Certainly, we find examples of all these familiar tropes in photographs of college and university classrooms—you will see them, too. But these familiar clichés are not the whole story. We also see teachers and students adapting and altering expectations for and uses of classrooms and technologies in ways that range from mundane workarounds to inspired innovations. We see the visual traces of the relationships between teaching and learning, and the physical space and technologies in and through which they occur, defined by "compromises, collisions, and unexpected outcomes" (Boys 2011, 35). More than anything, we see a future in which educators and learners deliberately embrace the possibility of entering learning spaces together, be they physical or virtual, with mutual transformation in mind.

As you encounter the photographs from a variety of postsecondary teaching and learning settings that follow, consider what aspects of space and technology stand out to you; how the people in them appear to use, adapt, or adapt to them; and to what extent they seem to support or hinder teaching and learning.

4.02
A faculty member in chemistry speaks to students in a chemistry class at a baccalaureate institution.

4.03
*A faculty member in
mechanical engineering
gestures to her presentation
in a thermal science class at a
doctoral institution.*

4.04
A faculty member in biology speaks with students during a biology class at an associate's institution.

4.05
Students in a religious studies class at a doctoral institution track a presentation projected to multiple locations in the classroom.

4.06
A graduate teaching assistant works with students during a physics recitation section at a doctoral institution.

4.07
A graduate student leads a chemistry study group at a doctoral institution.

4.08
*A faculty member in art
demonstrates a technique to a
student in a drawing class at
an associate's institution.*

Learning Spaces

Some learning spaces convey their purpose at a glance. In addition to painted and printed titles labeling rooms by department, we find easels in studio art, mineral specimens in geology, music stands in performance, and Bunsen burners in chemistry. In some cases, such as the science suite in image 4.04, the glass-walled classrooms also communicate institutional values and goals: the physical transparency of the learning space allows anyone walking by to view the activities, people, and learning happening inside. Creating a transparent space, it is hoped, leads to a transparent educational experience, in which students have ready access to learning opportunities, an understanding of their purpose, and an ability to see themselves doing science (Winkelmes, Boye, and Tapp 2019). But learning spaces are not obligated to tell us what they are for or why they matter; rather, educational spaces and the people who teach and learn within are in two-way relationships. Put another way, "we make the space and the space makes us" (Doorley and Witthoft 2012, 158), or in recent architectural thinking, "meaning-making occurs through the activation of space by our bodies . . . space and its occupation are not separate or in a behaviorist stimuli-response relationship, but endlessly informing and influencing each other" (Boys 2011, 6).

A ubiquitous kind of higher education space, the lecture hall, allows us to explore such relationships. An auditorium with fixed seats in rows, all facing forward, conveys certain structural messages: the teacher is in charge; students' attention belongs at the front of the room; students generally stay seated and have little need for interaction. Such messages can be as frustrating for teachers as they are oppressive for students. One STEM instructor at a bachelor's institution felt trapped: "I'm limited in how far I can move because of the setup. I spend a lot of time at the podium because that's where the computer is. . . . The little slice of chalkboard between screen and podium is where I do most of my writing." Another STEM professor from a doctoral institution put their frustration this way: "From the student's perspective, I'm dwarfed by the slide and screen. In my mind, I always think 'there's the professor.' In reality, 'there's the slide!' . . . I hate it for teaching. It looks like a movie theater—big screen, passive learning. . . . Ideally, it's less about me and more about students interacting." While fixed seats and huge screens may not communicate an educational ideal, in *The Teaching and Learning Project* photographs, what instructors and students decide to do in a space often dances with such expectations in unexpected ways—sometimes in alignment, sometimes at odds, rarely static. As you view the next group of images, notice how teachers and students work within and around the messages conveyed by the space: are they conforming, rebelling, or adjusting? How can you tell?

4.09
A faculty member in chemistry annotates a presentation during a chemistry class at a doctoral institution.

4.10
A student in the back of a chemistry class at a doctoral institution raises a hand to ask a question.

4.11
A faculty member in chemistry engages students in small group discussion during a large chemistry class at a doctoral institution.

4.12
Students in a large chemistry class at a doctoral institution engage in small group discussion.

The question of our physical presence—of human bodies together in a room, for the purpose of learning—is an important one. How we position ourselves and relate physically in classrooms carries and creates meaning, value, and power. As bell hooks reflected:

> Teachers may insist that it doesn't matter whether you stand behind the podium or the desk, but it does. I remember in my early teaching days that when I first tried to move out from behind the desk, I felt really nervous. I remember thinking, "This really is about power. I really do feel more 'in control' when I'm behind the podium or behind the desk than when I'm walking toward my students, standing close to them. . ." Acknowledging that we are bodies in the classroom has been important for me, especially in my efforts to disrupt the notion of professor as omnipotent, all-knowing mind. (1994, 138)

In *Teaching to Transgress*, hooks shared these thoughts in dialogue with philosopher Ron Scapp, who responded to the idea of teachers occupying space in less hierarchical ways: "You bring with you a certain kind of potential. . . . As we come physically close, suddenly what I have to say is not coming from behind this invisible line. . . . As people move around it becomes more evident that we work in the classroom" (138). Moreover, we engage in shared work in the classroom, teachers and students alike—a quality that contributes to the classroom as "a location of possibility" (207).

Take another moment to sit with the images on the preceding pages. What do you feel when the professor is far away and students are passive? When she is close by and engaged? When she is somewhere else, and students' peer-to-peer interactions are in focus? Certainly, the room, along with the technology, shaped aspects of what happened in this classroom, but the temporary occupants have also found ways around and between its constraints, arranging themselves to engage, learn, and subvert some of the expectations about teaching and learning built into the space itself. (Note that photographs 4.09 – 4.12 and associated prompts for observation and reflection are included in the online resource "Close Reading and Observation Exercises."

On college and university campuses today, the act of "breaching" (Boys 2011, 173) the apparent expectations of the physical space holds particular significance. Evidence about what forms of teaching best promote learning in higher education has grown markedly over the past several decades. From an educational research perspective, it is now clear: well-implemented teaching methods that engage students in some form of interactive or collaborative work in the classroom—on their own or interspersed with segments of lecture—tend to result in increased learning, often with quantitatively larger benefits for marginalized students, such as those with identities and backgrounds disproportionately excluded from higher education (Theobald et al. 2020; Freeman et al. 2014). Researchers propose a variety of mechanisms for the documented effectiveness of this family of active learning methods, including helping students connect new learning to what they already know, prompting students to practice recall and application of concepts, and enhancing a sense of belonging (Ambrose et al. 2010).

Over the past several decades, colleges and universities have been designing and building some classrooms with active learning in mind; these spaces often have moveable tables and chairs, allowing student groups to gather around tables facing one another. They may not have a single, fixed room orientation, and they allow teachers to move among groups of students. But research suggests it is not the space itself that improves learning; rather it is what happens inside that matters (Stoltzfus and Libarkin 2016). That is not to say that learning spaces are inconsequential; in fact, room setup may contribute to shifting teachers' methods and beliefs, as well as to institutional efforts to change the overall culture of teaching and learning (Talbert and Mor-Avi 2019). Whether supported by the

format of the learning space or in contrast to it, the choices of the people in the learning spaces are crucial.

Due to the relatively long lifetime of built environments like classrooms, instructors and students entering today's and tomorrow's learning spaces, redesigned or not, may need to work purposefully against the physical forms and arrangements that they find. Moreover, during a day in the life of a typical college classroom, a single room may host lectures, discussions, student group projects, adjunct faculty office hours, student club meetings, and faculty or administrative committee meetings. It will host these functions regardless of what is inside, and

4.13
A faculty member in mathematics assists students during a large mathematics class at a doctoral institution.

except for those classes with specialized or unique equipment, how the room is used will be based largely on the implicit or deliberate choices of people who attend.

Borrowing a term from computer science and popular culture, chemistry professor John Pollard found purpose in implementing intentional classroom "hacks" at the University of Arizona. Starting out, Pollard tried to implement active, collaborative strategies in crowded lecture halls, but found that the "classroom space was working against me." When trying to circulate among students, he and the instructional team could not interact with most of the students due to the layout (John Pollard, interview with author, December 7, 2020). Pollard worked with colleagues on campus to find alternatives and ended up collaborating with the library, technology support, the teaching and learning center, and the provost to take over a large, open space with temporary equipment and pilot a new format. Echoing bell hooks's reflections, Pollard describes his early days teaching there:

> I brought my entire class in there one day; there were pillars with temporary monitors on them, rented round tables everywhere, and screens set up around the room. I remember the first day of class in that space—it was such a different experience to be in the center of this huge group of students. I put the microphone on and remember feeling very uncomfortable, thinking "this was a bad idea," but it worked well. The ability to sit at a table with students, to be on the same level, completely changed my engagement with students. It's like eating together and having a great conversation that you don't want to stop; it has transformed what it means to gather students together. (Interview with author, December 7, 2020)

Pollard's creative ways around the limitations of traditional learning spaces sparked enthusiasm for changing not only classroom methods, but the entire

undergraduate chemistry curriculum. The institution eventually took note of the impressive results and created over forty redesigned active learning class-rooms (Talanquer and Pollard 2017). Pollard explains the long-lasting impacts on teachers, too: "Space matters. It's been the most effective and transformative tool to help faculty move toward evidence-based instruction. Suddenly instead of working against you, the space is working with you" (interview with author, December 7, 2020). Changing the space does not lead directly to changes in teaching, but rather, an array of complex interactions; altered learning spaces may express changing beliefs of teachers and students, advance commitments

4.14
A faculty member in music conducts during a music class at a doctoral institution.

to equity and inclusion, mobilize interest in exploring educational approaches, and support long-term adoption of new methods, even in the face of challenges (Knaub et al. 2016; Mulcahy, Cleveland, and Aberton 2015; Strijbos, Kirschner, and Martens 2004).

Through photographs of learning spaces, we have started to see them not so much as the walls, chairs, items, surfaces, and arrangements within, but as starting points for choices made by instructors and students together. The process of re-designing learning spaces is as important as the results.

4.15
A faculty member in applied behavior analysis at a doctoral institution conducts a discussion-based class outside.

4.16
A faculty member in sociology conducts a class in an outdoor courtyard at a doctoral institution.

Connecting through Technology

Technology can be novel and exciting, even in higher education, but at the core it should be useful. Postsecondary instructors may have access to a wide variety of things—ranging from physical items like erasable chalkboards and whiteboards, to digital devices like computers and tablets, to online applications and platforms like learning management systems and simulation software—each with characteristics that enable and even prompt certain kinds of usefulness when employed to support learning, sometimes called "affordances" (Strijbos, Kirschner, and Martens 2004). As Derek Bruff aptly put it, "We should be intentional in how we use technology, looking for ways the technology can support student learning" (2019, 2).

We see in the photographs of *The Teaching and Learning Project* examples of classroom technological environments that are layered and nuanced. Sometimes, frankly, they're a mess—dangling and tangled cords, old-school overhead projectors next to high-tech digital screens, and different generations of technology in the foreground and distance, with ubiquitous coffee cups and water bottles regularly endangering old and new devices. In one of the images that follows (4.17), a student works at a chalkboard while referring to a smartphone. Did the instructor ask students to bring their smartphones to the board? Possibly, but it seems just as likely that the chalkboard was there, a built-in technology well suited for simultaneous collaboration, display, and spatial arrangement of many concepts and ideas, and smartphones were a familiar way of accessing information beyond the room. Teachers and learners use what is intuitive and familiar in new combinations to get the job done, sometimes resulting in unexpected and seemingly awkward arrangements that nevertheless work.

In contrast, instructors may tend to avoid trendy or flashy classroom technologies that are too fussy and difficult to use in real teaching life. One institution

I know installed smartboards, combination computer and whiteboard devices mounted on walls, in dozens of classrooms, at not a small cost, and found that few instructors used them because they were hard to set up and operate—a pattern others have observed as well (Boys 2011, 97). Recall Lee Shulman's reflections on the complexity and near impossibility of teaching discussed in chapter 1, then add a finicky computer, a touch panel with multiple views controlling lights, screens, inputs, and outputs, and some new and unfamiliar software; it is easy to feel the potential for instructor and student overload. Attention is a commodity, and given the importance of focusing on student learning, we understand why technology use may be driven by what works most easily and reliably. For new technologies that have compelling features but take significant practice, instructors benefit from play spaces, both physical and virtual, away from students and outside of the teaching term, ideally supported by training, guidance, and access to instructional design and technology experts to answer their questions.

What we love the most in these learning-teaching-technology images are the moments where students are connecting over, around, and through technology. The reality in college and university classrooms is that students bring what they have, including different brands and models of phones, tablets, and laptops; instructors must be ready to make whatever learning activities they have work with that great variety, and institutions should provide technology to students who need it. As discussed in chapter 2, emotion plays a crucial role in learning; in order to be useful, technologies must be able to facilitate not only exchange of information, but also students' "affective encounters" (Boys 2011, 91). We often see sheets of paper—notes, worksheets, scratch paper—lending their reliable surfaces, ready for annotation and easy sharing alongside digital technologies.

As you interact with the photographs that follow, images 4.17 − 4.21, take special note of the technologies that you find in the foreground and background alike, how they are employed by students and teachers, and the connections between and among learners and instructors that you observe. (These photographs and prompts are included in the online resource "Close Reading and Observation Exercises.")

4.17
*Students share key points
from a group discussion
during a women's studies
discussion section at a doctoral
institution.*

4.18
Students use clickers to anonymously respond to questions during a physics class at a doctoral institution.

4.19
Students engage in various ways during an economics class at a doctoral institution.

4.20
Students engage in small group work during a chemistry class at a doctoral institution.

4.21
*Students work together during
an information systems and
technology class at a doctoral
institution.*

Distance and Disruption

My perception of these images has shifted since COVID-19. As campuses with significant in-person educational programs, including my own, moved all teaching and learning online, some of our most taken-for-granted technologies when on campus became our biggest challenges. In particular, the ease of working together on a shared surface (paper, chalkboard, screen), concurrent with the immersive communication of in-person interaction, was especially difficult to recreate with available online tools. We patched together software and equipment, shipping items to students and arranging no-contact pickup for instructors as needed; we were fortunate to be able to do so, as this financial investment was not feasible in all institutions and regions. Students turned to non-educational messaging and collaboration platforms from business, video gaming, and other sectors. Training for and discussions among instructors prompted sharing practices among many who had never before taught online. We found a way, but with far fewer of the affective encounters that make postsecondary learning the textured, supportive, and immersive experience we know and want it to be.

Of course, teachers have been teaching and students have been learning online for decades; the key disruption due to the COVID-19 pandemic was that, suddenly, the great majority had no other choice. In 2018, 35% of the over 19.6 million students enrolled in degree-granting postsecondary institutions in the United States took at least one distance course, typically delivered via online technologies (NCES 2019a, table 311.15). As colleges and universities are notoriously slow to change, going from about one-third of students studying some online to well over three-quarters of students studying mostly or completely online during the pandemic (Hess 2020) is an epic shift. Because online courses were historically offered less by some institutions than others, this change also caused institutions that had few or no online offerings before the pandemic to suddenly spin up the infrastructure to function fully online (Burns and McCormack 2020). It also means that quite a few faculty who had never taught a fully or partially online course did so in 2020-2021 (Lederman 2019, 2020).

The photographs of *The Teaching and Learning Project* explore various modes of distance learning, including those in the next group of images (4.22 – 4.26), which show courses with remote participants joining via videoconference and instructors teaching online from home, alongside their families, pets, and household activities. However, the full range of experiences with online education is not shown; these photos sample relatively privileged remote and home environments with adequate technology and internet service, which is not the case for many students and is an ongoing barrier to equity (Lederman 2020). As you contemplate these photographs, we ask you to hold in your mind, too, what is not in the frame: parents of young children, who may need to teach and learn from home while caregiving; students lacking personal computers; students with inadequate internet at home, struggling to access courses on mobile phones, sometimes studying in parking lots near free Wi-Fi signals. The downsides of distance education's flexibility and access include distraction, burnout, and inequity.

The Teaching and Learning Project photographs could inform the development of new educational technologies, as they highlight the distinct need for affective, personal connection. We need, for example, technologies that enable better eye contact during videoconferencing, applications that support multi-stream collaboration without forcing a choice between sharing emotion and sharing content, and ways to interact online that give participants the feeling of being part of a community, rather than the isolation of appearing as one of many tiny boxes. Those and other functions also need to be accessible across commonly used platforms, without expensive add-on equipment; until internet access becomes universally available regardless of income or geography, they must also not rely on excessive bandwidth. In a world where postsecondary teaching may be interrupted by natural disasters, more frequent severe weather due to climate change, and outbreaks of disease, knowing that teaching and learning can continue through adequate, effective technologies is more critical than ever.

4.22
*A remote guest speaker joins
a communications class at a
doctoral institution.*

4.23
*A faculty member in
management at a doctoral
institution prepares for
students in her project
management class to
collaborate remotely with
students from another
institution.*

4.24
A faculty member in business administration at a master's institution teaches online as her son works on his homework.

4.25–4.26
Sequence of two photographs: A faculty member in business administration at a master's institution teaches online.

Unstaging the Future

The Teaching and Learning Project encountered several spaces purposely made to stay unfixed, raw, and changeable, with elements designed to be transformed over and over again with and by students and educators. These spaces open up a potentially powerful vision for future postsecondary teaching space and technology.

Unlike the active learning classrooms discussed earlier, these rooms not only have moveable tables and chairs, but often have reconfigurable walls and partitions, feature flexible vertical and horizontal display areas for students' work, and may be set up with zones for different kinds of learning activities such as discussion, individual or small group work, use of computers or other equipment, and extended forms of physical making and exploration through models, artifacts, experiments, and prototypes. In the photographs that follow, images 4.27 – 4.31, these unstaged spaces were used for graphic design and architecture classes, though I have also been involved in the use of unconventional, blank slate learning spaces to explore new formats and modes of teaching in the social sciences and STEM fields, and they may be just as relevant in the humanities and other areas.

Having so many degrees of freedom in a learning environment may seem daunting. However, an unstaged space does not need to remain completely ambiguous—aspects can be temporarily fixed to support student exploration of new and more complex modes of thinking and discovery, as you see in the photographs of students interacting with each other and with work in progress. The difference is the intentionality: unstaged spaces may prompt instructors to make conscious decisions about configuration and technologies. They also allow for the possibility that some of those choices involve the current students. Such classrooms embody the complex interplay we have been exploring, almost requiring that the people involved in teaching and learning consider themselves as physical beings and humans in relationship; that they help shape the space and technology; and that the space and technology in turn activate and support their learning and discovery. Unstaged spaces make it clear that "learning activities are . . . about more than the space; . . . Space is . . . about more than just the learning activities" (Boys 2011, 85). They are also well suited to the gradual untethering of technology through greater wireless access and modularity that we are experiencing in the twenty-first century, and they make room for a future of as-yet-unknown developments in the research on learning. No classroom can make learning happen, but perhaps we can think of radically flexible spaces as important and purposeful parts of the ecosystem of higher education classrooms and technologies.

4.27–4.28
Sequence of two images: A faculty member in graphic design facilitates critique during a typography class at a doctoral institution.

4.29
Students work independently during a typography class at a doctoral institution.

4.30
*Students work independently
during a design class at a
doctoral institution.*

4.31
*Students listen to peer
presentations during a design
class at a doctoral institution.*

Questions for Further Reflection

- As you reflect on the spaces in which you teach, consider what you think these spaces communicate or imply about the nature of teaching and learning. To what extent has your teaching aligned with, adapted to, or breached the apparent expectations built into the space?
- Think of a time when your use of technology in teaching seemed particularly effective or conducive to learning for your students. If you were to see photographs of that time, what might you notice about the way the technology was used?
- In what ways do educational development offerings at your institution assume that space dictates activities? In what ways do or could they encourage instructors to hack or breach the apparent expectations built into teaching spaces and technologies?
- Who makes decisions about teaching spaces and technologies at your institution? Are they informed by visual representations of current uses, alongside other data and evidence? How might such visual evidence complement the decision-making process?

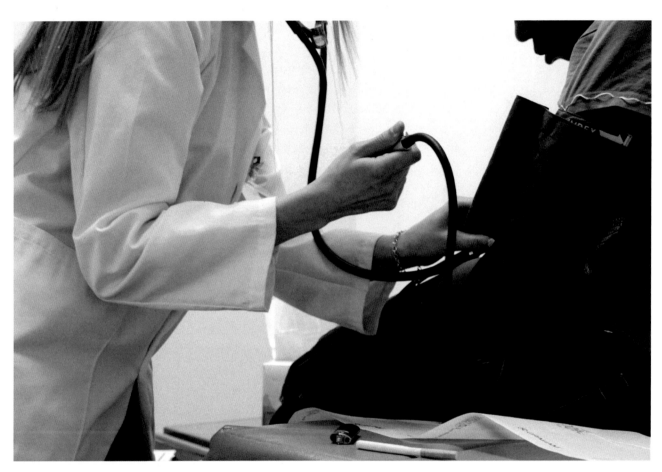

5.01

*A medical student at a doctoral institution works with a patient
at a free clinic as part of a service learning program.*

CHAPTER 5

Beyond Campus

Teaching and Learning in Context

Seasoned practitioners don't always . . . perform [like a] textbook. . . . Clinical skills, versus other knowledge, are best lived or learned in the clinic.

—*technical/professional instructor and participant in The Teaching and Learning Project, doctoral institution*

[The students] have an understanding of how their design has an impact on the people they are trying to help. . . . They know that these people have loved ones. . . . It's challenging, but if I could, I would definitely do this every semester.

—*STEM instructor and participant in The Teaching and Learning Project, doctoral institution*

Off the Campus Map

Through photographs in preceding chapters, we have visited and reflected on many of the places within college and university campuses where teaching and learning occur, including classrooms of many kinds, neat and chaotic alike. But a college or university is more than its campus, and learning extends well outside the lines of the campus map. Institutions are part of their communities; students and faculty learn and collaborate with nonprofit and civic organizations, K–12 schools, and a wide range of employers. As central as classroom-based learning is, these partnerships, when structured well, become crucial for postsecondary institutions and for their larger communities. Campus-community partnerships create new pathways for access to higher education and ensure that the education offered is authentic, relevant, and embracing of complexity.

As physical campuses emptied during the COVID-19 pandemic in 2020, the roles of physical campuses came into question; some argued against their ability to endure in their current forms (e.g., Taparia 2020; McKenzie 2019; DeVaney 2020). This questioning arrived alongside high-profile US institutional closures and consolidations in recent years, reflecting economic and demographic forces already straining finances within the higher education sector in the United States (Education Dive 2020; Butrymowicz and D'Amato 2020)—phenomena that are shared, to varying degrees, with institutions in the UK, Australia, and elsewhere that are facing enrollment disruptions and budget shortfalls due to the coronavirus pandemic (Witze 2020). In this chapter, as you see how postsecondary institutions intertwine with their communities through examples in the United States, it is an opportunity to reflect on and become clearer about the purpose of college and university campuses more broadly—not as isolated enclaves, but as organizations that support productive, contextual learning benefitting not just students, but also neighbors, families, institutions, businesses, and communities.

Learning in the Community

Learning that brings postsecondary students together with community partners, usually through structured coursework with guidance and mentorship from college or university faculty, has several names in the United States, including service learning, field-based experiential learning, and community-based learning. These approaches have been heralded as "high impact practices" due to their association with student success broadly, and more specifically for their contributions to deep learning, the kind where students "integrate, synthesize, and apply knowledge . . . understand themselves in relation to others and the larger world, and . . . acquire the intellectual tools and ethical grounding to act with confidence for the betterment of the human condition" (Kuh 2008, 17). It is no wonder that in recent years, such learning experiences have extended beyond settings where they were first implemented, such as health and education, to new applications including computer science hack-a-thons, urban studies projects, environmental fieldwork, and business and design projects (e.g., Lara and Lockwood 2016; Brail 2013).

This type of learning can help to resolve apparent tensions between the ideal of a liberal education and the practical need for career preparation. Community-based learning supports students' development of deep and broad critical thinking, grounded in real-world experiences, which are frequently among the intended outcomes of a liberal education; at the same time, US employers report being more likely to hire recent graduates with such experiences due to their confidence in the way these experiences contribute to employers' top-tier desired skills, including communication, critical thinking, ethical judgment, teamwork, and real-world applications (Hart Research Associates 2018). The positive impacts of community-based learning and service learning programs on student success in US higher education are well researched and extend to students' professional and social development (Trager 2020). Having engaged my own students in service learning, I can personally attest to those positive impacts (first-person statements in this chapter are in reference to Martin Springborg). For example, students in one of my photography courses could choose a service learning project teaching high school students about documentary photography. Those high school students could, as a result, incorporate photography into their volunteer work with younger kids and other organizations. Some of my most accomplished students took part in this and other service learning partnerships, and a few of them went on to transfer to prestigious universities. The rough diagram pictured in figure 5.02 illustrates how this train-the-trainer model worked with our institution, Inver Hills Community College (IHCC), connecting with a community partner,

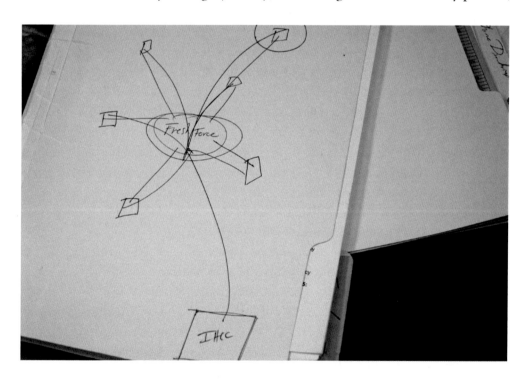

5.02
An impromptu illustration of a service learning program at an associate's institution.

5.03
Students in a sociology class at a doctoral institution serve at a community food shelf.

Fresh Force, which in turn coordinated volunteers at many school sites across the region.

Such positive impacts are also recognized by faculty and students at institutions across the United States. The national Campus Compact, the "only national higher education association dedicated solely to campus-based civic engagement," lists 1,022 member institutions, each providing community-based learning programs and opportunities (Campus Compact, n.d.). I've made photographs of service learning courses at several institutions. Some of these courses were especially fitting of one institution's Jesuit focus, where the service learning program is devoted to carrying out the mission of positive community involvement and impact; elsewhere, service learning courses enabled colleges and universities to connect with and contribute to their surrounding communities and engage students in applied learning.

In order to document service learning courses, I worked with staff from both centers for teaching and learning and well-established service learning programs. Many of my images from these courses illustrate the institutions' deep roots of service to the community and the rich learning experiences that emerge from those traditions; in some cases they are embedded across the curriculum. The images show engineering faculty and students visiting sites to evaluate their prototype designs in use by children with disabilities. They show students treating patients at a local free clinic. They show students preparing food and serving those in the community who are in need of a hot meal. The images emphasize human connections with community members that simply cannot be replicated or approximated within the physical borders of a campus. As you spend time with images 5.04 – 5.07, consider how the service part of the learning comes through in the photographs. (These photographs and prompts, with several others from this chapter, are included in the online resource "Close Reading and Observation Exercises.")

5.04–5.05
Sequence of two photographs: A faculty member in engineering at a doctoral institution works with her students at a community organization for children with disabilities, where children use adaptive learning tools designed by the students.

5.06
Medical students at a doctoral institution work with a patient at a free clinic as part of a service learning program.

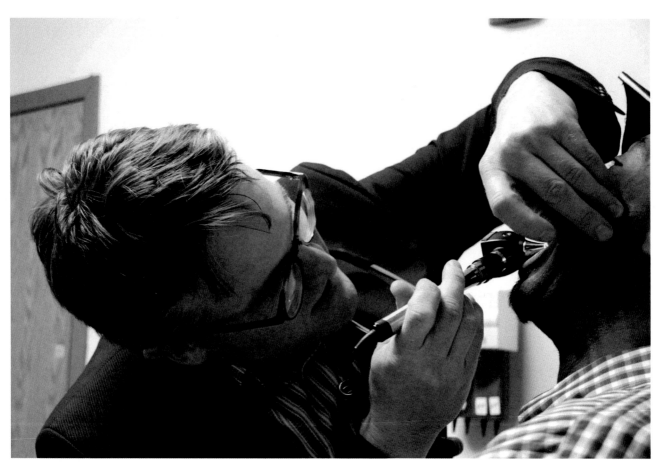

5.07
A faculty member in physician assistant studies at a doctoral institution with a patient at a free clinic as part of a service learning program.

There is much more going on than you might notice on first viewing these images. These service learning experiences entail more than committing to and providing service, and more than simply applying classroom or textbook ideas in new settings—they involve complex negotiations and networks of support. Students may be navigating new dimensions of their identities, for example, as future members of a profession. In an interview for *The Teaching and Learning Project*, one faculty member involved in guiding students' community-based learning observed: "Professionalism . . . it's something to talk about it, but another to practice it. Tools [and] uniforms mean something. Junior practitioners are wearing them, [others] are not." This instructor went on to reflect on the multiple layers of observing, modeling, and relationship-building happening in community-based settings: "Students get to see their own teachers practicing. . . . They listen to how their teachers interact with [community members], how they address their concerns [and] develop rapport. Sometimes that observation is better than hearing the teacher try to describe this."

Service and community-based learning also has the potential to support postsecondary students' exploration and integration of identity and values. At Caltech, the Center for Teaching, Learning, and Outreach found that students participating in community-based learning with local public K–12 schools not only gained skills in teaching, communication, and deeper understanding of their STEM studies, but also reported enhanced patience, reflection on their growth and change while in college, and awareness of unearned socioeconomic privileges that helped some of them succeed in STEM fields. Cassandra and colleagues understand these developments as part of the formation of students' identities, including their reflection on the social context for scientific learning and work, as well as the importance of partnership and collaboration with communities (Horii and Aiken 2013). Other institutions have purposefully embedded community engagement in courses within general education and various disciplines, such as one college's required ethics and diversity course, where this form of learning encouraged "connections between one's ethical values and one's actions in our diverse world" and "deeper engagement with the cultural, social, and other organizational systems that bind communities together" (Caldwell-O'Keefe and Recla 2020, 153).

Whether built into a course, or structured as a co-curricular activity, service and community-based learning benefit from careful incorporation of structures and methods that support equitable participation. Buffie Longmire-Avital's critical analysis of ways in which high impact practices can reproduce or disrupt longstanding higher education inequities offers important guidance. For example, Longmire documents multiple barriers to the participation of historically minoritized students, ranging from awareness of opportunities and their benefits, to financial and personal barriers, to ongoing systemic unconscious bias among instructors and mentors (Longmire-Avital 2018, 2019b). Community-engaged learning also needs instructors and mentors who are prepared to model critical reflection (Caldwell-O'Keefe and Recla 2020). Longmire-Avital articulates a model for critical mentoring that prioritizes mentors' own reflection on their positionality and privilege, along with the cultural wealth that historically minoritized students contribute, the potentially reparative impact of high impact practices on educational inequities, and the need for self-care for students and mentors alike (Longmire-Avital 2019a, 2020).

In addition to building these forms of instructor/mentor preparation and reflection into these experiences, fulfilling the potential of service and community-based learning also takes often unseen labor in the form of planning and follow-up work. Teachers of service learning courses often work closely with students before and after their interactions with community partners. As you see these interactions in the photographs, particularly in images 5.08 – 5.14, some may look much like other classroom-based learning. Notice if your encounter with the community components changes your perspective on those seemingly routine PowerPoint presentations and discussions, including the nature of the work of the faculty and students—the work behind the service learning. At times, these photographs capture moments when service learning students are being coached on-site by their faculty mentors, or when they are pausing to grapple with challenging issues and unfamiliar routines in these new-for-them community settings. In other cases, we get a glimpse of the collaboration and relationship-building that happens between postsecondary teachers and community partners, who must also invest time and effort with each other.

The preparation and follow-up, along with the long-term support for and connection between postsecondary institutions and service learning sites, are crucial for both the learning part and the service part of service learning. The second portion of that equation has not received nearly as much attention, with many fewer studies exploring the benefits and challenges for community-based organizations when they partner with postsecondary institutions. In studies that do so, though, the importance of true reciprocity and collaboration emerge as critical elements underlying the success of service and community-based learning programs, especially transparency, clarity, communication, and collaborative planning (Blouin and Perry 2009; Karasik 2020). Postsecondary instructors and community partners alike invest time, effort, and attention into creating and maintaining equitable partnerships, as well as in preparing students to conduct themselves in ways that are suitable to the specific community settings, while students are still learning what those roles entail and how to apply knowledge and skills from class to new environments. Staff and offices supporting service and community-based learning also support these efforts: for example, at Caltech, the staff at the center that coordinates educational partnerships cultivates campus–K-12 partnerships on a district-wide basis, ensuring that teachers' input and needs are built into the planning process and that postsecondary students are well prepared for their work with younger students. The behind-the-scenes work of college and university faculty and staff, in partnership with community-based organizations, is what drives these powerful connections; as with other infrequently seen aspects of higher education, this work is worth making more visible and tangible through photographs.

5.08
A faculty member in physician assistant studies at a doctoral institution consults with students at a free clinic as part of a service learning program.

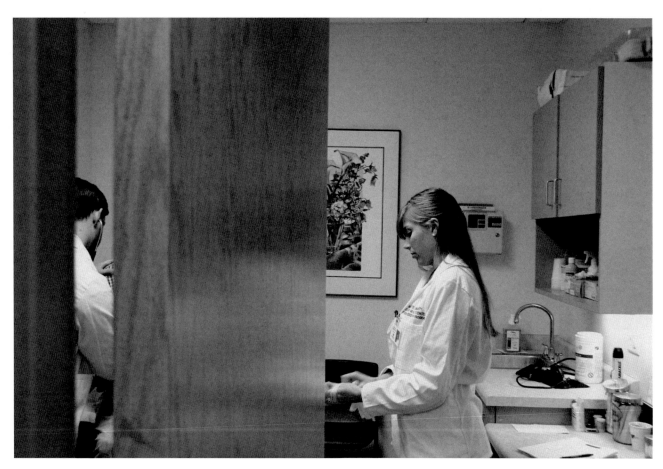

5.09
Medical students at a doctoral institution with a patient at a free clinic as part of a service learning program.

5.10
A faculty member in engineering at a doctoral institution reflects with engineering students during a discussion in a service learning class.

5.11
A faculty member in sociology at a doctoral institution answers questions from students following a campus presentation.

5.12
A faculty member in sociology at a doctoral institution gives a campus presentation on her research.

5.13–5.14
Sequence of two photographs: A faculty member in sociology at a doctoral institution consults with the director of a community food shelf as part of a service learning partnership.

Blurring the Boundaries

Higher education institutions in the United States are increasingly expanding learning beyond their campuses and beyond their typical students through programs that bring learning to students who might not otherwise have access, thereby lowering barriers to participation in college courses. Although online education may get more attention in this regard, concurrent and dual enrollment programs—both of which open college courses up to secondary school students, either at the secondary school site or elsewhere—have important roles to play (NACEP, n.d.).

I photographed dual enrollment classes at a technical college, and while some lines were clearly drawn to distinguish secondary school students' physical space within the college's culinary program, students otherwise largely worked and learned alongside each other in the sprawling, fully operational college kitchen, regardless of their age or enrollment status. I remember thinking as I photographed in this environment that this was a far cry from any learning experiences I had before college. Students exhibited significantly more professionalism and rigor in the interactions playing out before me, where they were ultimately responsible for the complete range of tasks required to staff, prepare, and serve banquet-style meals for events. The precision, teamwork, technical knowledge and skill development, and adoption of professional roles and comportment, among secondary and postsecondary students alike, stood out. As with any well-designed, complex college course—but one with added challenges of sourcing fresh ingredients, ensuring that banquet guests are served, and managing students at very different places in their educational trajectories—faculty invested substantial planning and behind-the-scenes work on logistics, not to mention the administrative and institutional commitment and coordination behind these hors d'oeuvres (see images 5.15 – 5.21).

5.15–5.16
Sequence of two photographs: A faculty member in culinary arts consults with culinary students at an associate's institution.

5.17
Space in a culinary arts kitchen is reserved for high school students at an associate's institution.

5.18–5.20
*Sequence of three photographs:
Students in a culinary arts
program at an associate's
institution prepare to serve
food for a campus event.*

5.21
Faculty in a culinary arts program at an associate's institution reflect on their work.

In addition to dual and concurrent enrollment, other kinds of programs also blur the lines between formal college enrollment and alternative settings, locations, and forms of access. For example, a collaboration between Columbus City Schools and Otterbein University has brought college and secondary teachers together through professional learning communities; along with other initiatives, this effort aims to build bridges between high school and university faculty and support students' transition to college (Otterbein University 2019). College-in-prison programs, where postsecondary faculty teach credit-bearing courses for incarcerated individuals working toward their degrees, are also reinventing what it means to be in college, while demonstrating positive impacts for participating students and reimagining justice in the US (Ken Burns Presents 2019; Fain 2019; Gerstmann 2019; Prison Studies Project, n.d.). As colleges and universities consider other communities where access to education is limited, newer programs are working to bring full-scholarship, academically rigorous liberal arts courses to isolated communities through partnerships with local community organizations (e.g., Bard Microcollege, n.d.). We hope that these examples, along with those shown in this chapter's photographs, spark expansive thinking about the locations, formats, and students we imagine when we picture higher education.

Whether higher education extends beyond the campus map through service and community-based learning, or whether the lines between college students and learners in the community become less distinct, postsecondary institutions are expanding the opportunities they provide. As we come to understand that a liberal arts education, which is fully compatible with technical and professional preparation, builds a more caring, compassionate, and civically engaged citizenry (AAC&U 2020), colleges and universities must continue to increase their contributions to their communities. After all, postsecondary institutions consist not only of students, faculty, and staff, but also of neighbors, job holders, leaders, volunteers, parents, and many other roles, right alongside community members. Ties are built on face-to-face, person-to-person experiences, which result in benefits not only to the community, but authentic learning for students, who will leave their postsecondary paths with the desire and ability to keep learning. We hope that they truly embrace the identity of a lifelong learner, due in part to their learning experiences outside the classroom and beyond the boundaries of the campus.

5.22
A faculty member in culinary arts prepares a table for a campus event.

Questions for Further Reflection

- What locations, formats, and students do you imagine when you picture higher education? How do the photographs in this chapter align with or challenge your conceptions?
- What do the photographs in this chapter communicate about the teaching practices and supports associated with service and community-based learning?
- If your campus includes service learning programs or opportunities, how are those activities made visible to people on campus? To people in the community? If photographs are present, or absent, in communications, why do you think that might be the case?

6.01
A faculty member in chemistry at a baccalaureate institution
assists students during office hours.

CHAPTER 6

Hidden Work

Educational Labor Revealed

My job can go from one end of the spectrum to the other, from crisis to amazing. Some days it's very very serious and others it's jumping for joy. [The photographs] captured both ends of the spectrum in one day—some photos where we're doing serious paperwork, others where we're happy and celebrating. I like seeing that range.

—*participant in The Teaching and Learning Project, baccalaureate institution, field not specified*

All faculty members must be properly supported financially, with appropriate job stability and support. They also should be affectively supported.

—*former dean, public university*

Sectors and Status

One of my earliest insights from the beginnings of *The Teaching and Learning Project* was the revelation of the many kinds of normally invisible work taking place on college and university campuses (first-person statements in this chapter are in reference to Martin Springborg). By photographing faculty, staff, and administrators in their offices, in centers for teaching and learning, in conference rooms, libraries, and casual campus spaces, the project began not only to burst typical university silos, but to cultivate empathy for and understanding of the educational labor undertaken by those filling the many different roles in postsecondary institutions today. The photographs also soon began to confront larger issues with contingent labor in higher education, such as the increasing numbers of adjunct faculty, with new immediacy.

When I first started formally making photographs for *The Teaching and Learning Project*—declaring it a project, describing it as such when asking people if they'd like to participate, and making sure participants gave informed consent for their inclusion in it—I was surprised at the number of "yes" responses I received; I had anticipated far more rejection. As much as I was an insider to various academic sectors, I perceived the walls of privacy to be high around my colleagues' work; it turned out that no one had ever asked.

I started by photographing my closest faculty colleagues, which led to conversations with and photographs of their deans, which led to conversations with and photographs of college provosts and presidents—all connected in some way to making sure teaching and learning could happen, and could continue to happen term after term, year after year. Not long after starting this project documenting postsecondary teaching and learning, I found I was dedicating just as much effort to documenting the hidden work of teaching, including the work of instructors beyond the classroom, and the work of administrators and aca-

6.02
An outline of an organizational chart at an associate's institution.

demic staff. This unexpected development showed the connectedness of major campus sectors to each other and to student success. We introduced you to some of these behind-the-scenes views as early as the introduction, and you may wish to go back to images 0.08 – 0.13 again, now observing with curiosity how these normally obscured views surface other dimensions of teaching that may be important. Likewise as you view the photographs in the next section, images 6.03 – 6.07, consider whether you have seen photographs documenting aspects of administrative and staff work that are necessary for the teaching and learning endeavors of instructors and students to continue, and what your experience, as well as the images, might mean. (Note that a selection of these photographs and prompts for reflection or discussion are included in the online resource "Close Reading and Observation Exercises.")

6.03
A book with notes on the lap
of an interim president at an
associate's institution.

6.04
*A student gets assistance from
the coordinator of a center for
international student services
at a baccalaureate institution.*

6.05
*The office doorway of the
coordinator of a center for
international student services
at a baccalaureate institution.*

6.06
Outside the office of a faculty member in engineering at a master's institution.

By photographing and talking with faculty colleagues and their deans, I was also introduced to many of the contingent faculty members working in various departments at my own institution, including part-time, adjunct, and non-tenure-track faculty. Due to the rise of part-time faculty appointments in the United States and given that part-time and full-time contingent faculty outnumber tenured and tenure-track faculty across the spectrum of institution types (AAUP 2018), students are very likely to be taught by adjunct or part-time instructors from the beginning of college—they are a crucial part of students' higher education experience. Yet, many contingent faculty struggle to make ends meet in the US and elsewhere. In Japan, part-time lecturers, whose numbers have risen in recent decades, often teach at multiple institutions simultaneously, yet still count among the country's working poor (Kimie 2021). The situation is similar in the US, where part-time adjunct instructors comprise at least 40% of all faculty (Douglas-Gabriel 2019) and where the vast majority, 89 percent as of 2014, teach at more than one institution (House Committee on Education and the Workforce 2014). As *The Teaching and Learning Project* expanded to institutions across the US, contingent faculty remained a strong focus of the work. Given their sheer numbers, it makes sense that *The Teaching and Learning Project* features many contingent and part-time faculty doing impressive work—in teaching, service, and scholarship. Beyond their ubiquitous presence, though, two things stand out: first, their vital role is often misunderstood by their own full-time and tenure-track faculty colleagues. Second, perhaps as a result, students often misperceive the role and importance of part-time and contingent faculty, especially if students are able to observe distinct differences in an institution's engagement with or recognition of faculty according to employment status. This epidemic of misunderstanding and under recognition is playing out in the US in debates citing, for example, falsehoods such as the subversion of the professoriate by part-time hires (Scott 2020), which fail to recognize that contingent faculty are often doing the best they can to serve students, with few resources and many hurdles. Similar lack of support and struggles are likewise documented among sessional instructors in Australia, New Zealand, the European Union, and the United Kingdom (Harvey 2017).

Leora Baron-Nixon gives sage advice to colleges and universities in their employment and engagement of part-time faculty. With an eye toward student success, she affirms that "to provide, support, or sustain quality educational programs, all faculty members need to be part of their institution's creative, intellectual, and administrative fabric. To meet the challenge, an institution should create and foster an organizational climate and culture that are . . . inclusive" of all faculty. She goes on to describe an ideal state in which "the roles of all faculty who are engaged in teaching are identical" and "nonteaching roles of teachers, such as participation in institutional life, student advising, and professional contributions, are expected from and valued by all" (Baron-Nixon 2007, 15). The photographs of contingent faculty in *The Teaching and Learning Project* convey the ways in which part-time and contingent faculty members' engagement with students, dedication to teaching, and participation in the life of the institution are as vibrant and crucial as those of their tenure-track colleagues. Yet, the photographs also highlight that these contributions are often made without dedicated office space or job security, through office hours in borrowed corners and briefly empty classrooms, while teaching dizzying schedules of classes at multiple institutions and online, in some cases alongside other jobs. I hope that seeing these contributions and difficulties lends a new urgency to calls for action to support non-tenure-track faculty more substantively and effectively. Academic staff, too, may feel their contributions to the life of teaching and learning in their institutions are hidden and underrecognized, yet in so many ways, the work of higher education could not happen without them, and *The Teaching and Learning Project* makes those contributions undeniably real. In the United States, the term "staff" typically includes non-teaching roles, ranging widely across institutional functions: groundskeeping, information technology, residential support, accounting, and more. Academic staff members, as we will use the term within a US context, then, are non-faculty employees whose work is connected closely with academics: e.g., educational developers, librarians, administrative support personnel who organize and support other aspects of teaching such as scheduling, enrollment, and financial aid, and in some cases, depending on their self-identification, staff members in student affairs who work closely with students on academic support such as tutoring, coaching, and advising.

Academic staff tend to work in a liminal domain—a "betwixt and between" existence (Little and Green 2012) that defies clear role definitions and boundaries. On a practical level, academic staff may or may not hold secondary, part-time faculty appointments and they are often not included in governance and institutional decision-making, yet they work directly with students and teachers, supporting and contributing to the institution's educational goals. They frequently find themselves "in the uncomfortable space between the administration and the faculty, carrying out the edicts of the former while trying to appease the latter" (Bessette 2020). Educational developers, a subset of this larger set of academic staff, often serve as a crucial "link between . . . disciplinary academics, academic leaders, administrators, national research project members, graduate teaching assistants, doctoral students, and other academic developers," despite holding sometimes precarious and overlapping identities (Sutherland 2015, 209).

In the group of photographs that follows, images 6.08 – 6.16, part-time, full-time, adjunct, and tenure-track faculty, along with academic staff members, are shown engaged in various aspects of their work, some of which are rarely seen in images. How do the possibly contingent and liminal statuses of adjunct or part-time faculty and academic staff appear to you in these photographs? In what ways are those statuses visible or invisible?

6.07
A faculty member in engineering at a master's institution works in his office at the end of the day.

6.08
A faculty member in history at a baccalaureate institution meets with a student in an unused classroom.

6.09
*A faculty member in English
at a baccalaureate institution
quickly stops in his office
between classes.*

6.10
Faculty in biology hold a departmental meeting at a doctoral institution.

6.11–6.12
Sequence of two photographs: Faculty in philosophy meet as a department at an associate's institution.

6.13
A director of a center for teaching and learning at a doctoral institution consults with a teaching assistant.

6.14
A staff member in a center for teaching and learning at a doctoral institution conducts a session for faculty and graduate students during a teaching certificate program.

6.15
A director of a center for teaching and learning at a doctoral institution conducts a teaching consultation with a faculty member.

6.16
A librarian at a master's institution retrieves items from the institution's archives.

Misperceptions about contingent faculty and staff are perhaps matched by misperceptions about higher level administrative leaders and the function of administration more broadly in supporting teaching and learning. In the United States, deans, provosts, presidents, and various vice, associate, and assistant versions of those positions, and in some cases directors and other roles, are counted among an institution's administration, and are generally charged with supporting, funding, evaluating, organizing, and improving teaching and learning, depending on the role. A lack of knowledge about colleagues' work and contributions to the teaching and learning endeavor across campus sectors frequently leads to breakdowns in communication and trust between administrators, faculty, and staff, yet communication and trust are two essential elements for people working together toward a common goal like student success.

This erosion of community in postsecondary institutions may be exacerbated by ever-growing changes to the faculty and staff workforce, such as the increase in part-time and contingent faculty and the addition of mid-level administrators (Kezar, DePaola, and Scott 2019). These changes can have a direct and negative impact on long-standing higher education structures, such as faculty shared governance. Kezar, DePaola, and Scott note that "these various trends taken together create a very different kind of academic community than has existed at any time in the past. Faculty and staff are turning over in their roles more than ever and are largely unavailable given their contingent and outsourced status. And interactions among faculty and staff are likely to be tainted by their low morale, declining satisfaction, and overall feelings of disengagement" (2019, 95).

Alongside these negative consequences, though, mid-level administrators are often needed to ensure that institutions comply with increasingly complex national and regional regulations. Ideally, such administrators also provide vital support to faculty and students, though their roles may be perceived as detracting from, rather than supporting, those playing a more direct instructional role. In a similarly complicated way, contingent faculty may allow institutions to respond to changing student interests and enrollments more nimbly, even as their growing numbers raise concerns about instability, low pay, and lack of support. Despite these complexities, *The Teaching and Learning Project* frequently found members of all these groups to be highly engaged and dedicated—not "unavailable" at all, though not as connected as they could be, either. The community aspect of postsecondary work—creating an environment in which trust is maintained—is essential, and while imperfect, shows up in the efforts to connect across roles in the photographs. In images 6.17 – 6.23, what connections and disconnections between and among administrators, faculty, and staff stand out to you?

6.17
*Doors to the offices of the vice
provost and general counsel at
a doctoral institution.*

6.18
A dean of allied health at an associate's institution speaks to a colleague during a staff meeting.

6.19
A dean of allied health assists an emergency medical technician student at an associate's institution.

6.20-6.21
Sequence of two photographs: A president at an associate's institution facilitates an interdepartmental meeting of staff and faculty.

6.22
*An interim president at an
associate's institution facilitates
an interdepartmental meeting
of staff and faculty.*

6.23
A vice president for academic and student affairs at an associate's institution talks with staff in enrollment services.

Three Perspectives on Supporting Teaching

In an effort to provide a first-hand account of hidden work in higher education, I talked with three US college administrators who agreed to frank interviews provided their names not be used (personal communications with Martin Springborg, February 11, 2020 – March 9, 2020). They included a community college president, a community college vice president of academic affairs (a role equivalent to provost at many institutions in the US, or a deputy vice-chancellor in the UK), and a former college dean in a large public university. I asked each of them to address a common set of questions about their career path, institutional roles, and how current issues related to teaching in postsecondary education play out in their work. Prior to their current roles, they held a variety of tenure-track and contingent faculty appointments and administrative appointments in academic affairs, grants and research, technology, and online education. They represent administrative roles that traditionally work the most closely with faculty and provide support for teaching and learning. In elucidating the nature of hidden educational labor, these three administrators focused on why, how, and from whom their work and that of faculty and staff remains hidden; often-overlooked financial and workload burdens; and how to remedy these issues.

Hidden Work

These administrators shared revealing perspectives on the hidden nature of their own work, as well as that of faculty and staff. Certain aspects of teaching and supporting students only became visible as their roles evolved. The president explained that "as I got further into my career, I started to get curious about other things that impacted students. . . . It challenged my ideas of my responsibility and where that ended." The same president noted, "When I moved into [a] dean role, [I] had more of an appreciation for the resources everyone needs to teach well," and later, "as a [vice president I addressed] more questions, like how do you measure the value of what you do . . . and how do you measure the impact of [academic] programs?" Finally, "As president, [I'm] dealing with [the] board of trustees, policies, marketing and branding the institution, [and] legislators." This president also realized how hard it is to retain the perspectives that were so close earlier in their teaching career, noting that "I have to work hard every day to keep [the] pulse of students" and regretting being "more detached from faculty than I'd like to be."

It is striking how obscured each of these roles are from the views of virtually any other stations in postsecondary education; in parallel, photographs like those in images 6.26 – 6.29, showing closed-door administrative meetings, are very rarely portrayed publicly, contributing to these obscured perceptions of administrative work. The VP of academic affairs articulated more hidden administrative work in efforts to better support students: "It's amazing how fast the institution has needed to change. A lot of that is on the shoulders of the upper leadership of an institution." Despite the effort needed to make major changes, this administrator also lamented that "there really isn't any awareness of higher education administration as work. [Administrators] have been portrayed . . . as guys in the office with a cigar—some kind of upper echelon of the institution with not a lot of accountability," when nothing could be further from the truth. The VP of academic affairs noted wryly that "as a dean, you often have responsibility and accountability, but not authority."

All three were acutely concerned about the under recognition of contingent faculty and academic staff at their institutions. Broadly, the president explained that "people who are drawn to higher education already have a passion for student learning and success. It would be great if we could recognize more people for what they do and support them. . . . We could do a better job recognizing peoples' talents and gifts and ability to help students succeed."

Two of the interviewees noted structural divides between contingent and tenure-track faculty. Pointing out that most faculty governance roles are held by tenure-track faculty, the VP of academic affairs observed that "faculty leadership makes decisions that are in the best interest of full-time faculty." The president voiced additional dividing lines between full-time and part-time faculty, who "are in different bargaining units. . . . I think this needs to be fixed. It would build relationships across the college if there were more opportunities for these two groups to come together. Currently, part-time faculty are not invited to the table—to full-time faculty conversations"; part-time faculty "also get invited to other things on campus, but often those events are scheduled at times our part-time faculty cannot attend."

Concern about public perception of educational labor (or lack thereof) was also evident. The former dean remarked that "the mass media . . . tends to misunderstand the nuances of the college experience for both faculty members and students. . . . Faculty members are often portrayed as having easy careers, with light and easy workloads, guaranteed jobs, high pay, and a similar lack of responsibility." They also pointed out that "in the popular media, the work and issues of the part-time and/or adjunct faculty member receives little to no attention. This lack of attention probably stems from the same ignorance. . . . As with any labor issue, greater visibility is likely to result in positive change." As *The Teaching and Learning Project* has done for other hidden dimensions of higher education, we hope that the photographs contribute to this type of change.

6.24
*A provost and vice president
of academic affairs at an
associate's institution works in
her office.*

6.25
A dean of allied health at an associate's institution walks to her office between meetings.

6.26
*Staff and administrators from
several different offices meet at
a doctoral institution.*

6.27
A president consults with a staff member at an associate's institution.

6.28
A whiteboard during a budget meeting at an associate's institution.

6.29
A president and chief financial officer at an associate's institution talk before a faculty shared governance meeting.

Workload and Finances

These administrators had much to say about the intertwined problems of over-work and institutional finances, both of which function as additional hidden factors complicating the labor required to teach in postsecondary institutions. The former dean explained that "the current crisis seems to center on cost, return on investment for both students and society, and who should be financing a higher education. This focus requires institutions to be very cautious about the use of their fiscal resources, which sometimes results in an over-reliance on faculty members who are part-time or adjunct." Also recognizing the injustice in relying on contingent instructors, the same former dean explained that "I have seen too many faculty members in the last twenty years or so that have had a very hard time making ends meet, through no fault of their own . . . because the institution would not hire them full-time—would not create a necessary position."

The VP of academic affairs traced how institutional finances contribute to overwork: "We have a low rate of pay for adjuncts and faculty. These employees, as a result, keep up-taking work: overloads [and] working at other institutions in addition to their regular workload. It's a challenge for any institution to find . . . the resources to pay faculty enough to keep them from needing to do this." The president also explained that for academic work in their state, "there is no maximum workload. If the employee wants to work sixty hours [per week], they are allowed . . . so quality vs. quantity is a problem." This overwork also detracts from the ability of institutions to break down silos and cultivate leadership from within; as this president explained, "Because faculty are teaching so much, it is harder for them to branch out into other aspects of the institution, [such as] accreditation efforts [and] administrative functions." The VP of academic affairs testified to these challenges existing on top of an already increased expectation for faculty work, with a "notable progression in the amount of work administration expects of faculty over and above their teaching load." Counter to the public perception that faculty have it easy, many are on a trajectory of intractably increasing workloads, fueled by troubled financial support for higher education.

Strategies for Change

The administrators I spoke with were highly engaged in thinking about and enacting changes to help reveal hidden aspects of postsecondary educational labor in multiple ways. The college president worked to ensure recognition for adjunct faculty through events: "We have great adjuncts. 90 percent have been with us for more than ten years. I give a talk at a special dinner we have for them. Every fall, we get together and talk about contracts, engagement (with them, with the college), and highlight the things they are doing." The VP of academic affairs shared that faculty governance "is slowly changing—more adjuncts are represented in faculty shared leadership roles."

Others focused on redefining roles to better meet modern needs in the higher education sector. The former dean had given this substantial thought: "The traditional tenure-track appointment of faculty members is important in meeting the goals of teaching, research, and service, but these faculty members can require a commitment from the institution that may not most appropriately meet the needs of either the institution or the students. We are starting to see more institutions hiring faculty members who are concentrated on teaching, with a lesser emphasis on research and service, yet still hired full time and with opportunities for promotion. This is a positive step." Communication and shared planning can also play important roles in improving the environment for postsecondary teachers. This president shared one such approach for engaging faculty across appointment types, as well as staff, in the future of the institution: "I introduced the college to a one-year conversation process that . . . will focus on big questions including: What organizational structure do we need to achieve the results our students need to be successful? What roles and positions are needed or not needed? How will we educate? When? Where? What will we teach?" While participating in strategic conversations like these takes time, it also has the potential to bring forth that same passion for student learning and success that the president also noted as a hallmark of those drawn to working in higher education, and it can build a truly shared investment across roles in forward-looking, creative, and strategic planning.

Questions for Further Reflection

As you review the photographs in this chapter and throughout the book, as well as those you find online and in publications about higher education from your own institution and elsewhere, consider the work you observe in each frame:

- What signs or symbols show you, or hide from you, whether those doing the work are faculty, staff, or administrators?
- Can you tell which students are taught by contingent or tenure-track, part-time or full-time faculty?
- Where do you find evidence of silos being broken down or enforced, and a sense of community and collaboration being eroded or fostered?
- What other insights emerge for you about the nature of postsecondary educational work, hidden and revealed?

7.01
A faculty member in art at an associate's institution surveys the installation of The Teaching and Learning Project work in the college art gallery. (Reproduced by permission from Luke Austin.)

CHAPTER 7

Photographs and Change Agents

Campus Communities Encountering Themselves

If people only thought we could dare look at ourselves.
—*Dorothea Lange (1964)*

Defining Change

Throughout this book, we have explored ways in which photographs both reflect and have the potential to improve higher education. Anne Whiston Spirn discovered this same "synergy" between "the observing and portraying of the world and acting to change it" (Spirn 2008, xiii) in the work of photographer Dorothea Lange, who was herself aware of the possibilities when we "dare look at ourselves" (Spirn 2008, 8). Contemporary photographers such as Dawoud Bey have broken new ground in intending for photographs to exist "in conversation with communities," as he did with an exhibit of high school student portraits alongside the words of those portrayed, which "influenced curators and educators to consider how their work could have a greater impact" (Shakur 2018).

Of course, disciplines such as the fine arts, art history, design, journalism, and communications have long histories of employing, researching, creating, and integrating photographs into theory and practice. Documentary photographs have also played crucial roles in social change processes almost since the invention of the medium (Tate n.d.; Hostetler 2004). However, the use of documentary photography as an intentional and integrated strategy for systemic change of educational institutions and practices themselves is still relatively new for higher education. This chapter documents ways in which postsecondary institutions have so far leveraged the intrinsic properties and power of photographs to support their efforts to improve teaching, learning, campus climate, and other facets of their educational endeavors.

Colleges and universities have been grappling with the need for and process of organizational change for decades, with increasing urgency. Institutions around the world are examining change processes related to student access and success (Geertsema and van der Rijst 2021), sustainability practices within colleges and universities (Hoover and Harder 2015), and the role of educational developers in change processes (Gachago et al. 2021; Fossland and Sandvoll 2021). In the United States, as shortcomings persist, such as inadequate graduation rates, mounting educational debt, and inequities that are particularly harmful to marginalized students, national organizations and initiatives focused on studying, accelerating, and fostering major systemic changes have emerged (ASCN, n.d.; American Academy of Arts & Sciences 2017; NASEM, n.d.). To quote from the vision statement of one such endeavor, these efforts are bringing educators together so that "students in every institutional setting experience teaching that aligns with what we know about how people learn, and that draws in and supports all students," with coordinated projects helping to "integrate what is known and soon to be discovered about organizing, leading, and evaluating change efforts to maximize the individual and collective efforts" of those involved (ASCN, n.d.).

Broader recognition has emerged that isolated actions at individual institutions do not tend to shift the larger cultures and systems enough. Some projects have focused on identifying "levers" for change—actions that might have an outsized impact compared to the effort, backed by evidence from various academic disciplines (Laursen 2019). The higher education community is also becoming clearer about terminology and tools, defining a "change agent" as a person or group working to shift instructional practices, a "change practice" as a tactic or method to foster improvement, and a "change strategy" as a coherent, systematic plan (Henderson, Beach, and Finkelstein 2011). In this framework, creating and sharing photographs is one change practice that is beginning to be employed by change agents. What change strategies are guiding such use?

This chapter provides answers to that question in the form of intentional strategies that led to the photographs you have encountered throughout this volume and intentional strategies that leveraged those photographs to further advance institutional change priorities. Many of the changes, both intended and observed, are related to the culture of teaching and learning within higher education communities. Indeed, it is often "the goal of a to modify culture in particular ways, in order to support meaningful change" (Reinholz and Apkarian 2018, 3). Culture consists of people's identities, relationships, implicit and explicit messages about worth, structures of power, and traditions. Change agents look to culture because it is pervasive and may be unconscious for those who have lived and worked within a context for a long time. Changing practices without changing culture leads to a high likelihood of those new practices falling by the wayside, as unsupported and unintegrated add-ons without clear value, making changes to teaching culture a "wicked problem" (Sagy, Hod, and Kali 2019).

Institutions that hosted *The Teaching and Learning Project* both intended and observed changes in the culture of teaching. We include reflections from change agents at seven of the twenty-one campuses that have participated in *The Teaching and Learning Project*, including contributions from Cassandra Volpe Horii, co-author of this book, in her former capacity as assistant vice provost and director of the Center for Teaching, Learning, and Outreach (CTLO) at Caltech. The other six contributors and their contexts are as follows:

- Karishma Collette, assistant director, Center for Research on Learning and Teaching at the University of Michigan: This center used photographs to help launch the University of Michigan foundational course initiative, which was "a multi-year large course transformation project sponsored by the president's office" with the "aim to support the success of all students from a wide range of backgrounds and motivations, and to increase instructor satisfaction and joy in the teaching of large introductory courses" (document emailed to authors, August 2, 2019).
- Larkin Hood, associate research professor in the Schreyer Institute for Teaching Excellence, Penn State University: This large university system has twenty-four campus locations across the state, with the research-focused University Park flagship campus often receiving more attention than others;

photographs from "campuses other than University Park helped make the work of faculty at the campuses more visible to the greater university community," culminating in an exhibit of the photographs (document emailed to authors, January 30, 2020).

- Simon Huelsbeck, faculty member and division leader in studio art, Rochester Community and Technical College: This institution is a member of Minnesota State, the third largest system of state colleges and universities in the US, where the scale of the system can lead to faculty feeling disconnected from system-wide initiatives. Martin photographed Huelsbeck's class and shadowed the interim president; the visit culminated in a photographic exhibit (document emailed to authors, January 14, 2020).

- Sara Kacin, assistant provost for faculty development and faculty success and director of the Office of Teaching and Learning, and Mathew Ouellett, former associate provost and director of the Office of Teaching and Learning (later at Cornell University), Wayne State University: "We planned an itinerary that included meeting with staff to talk about consultations, visiting and photographing classes across the disciplines, and headlining our annual Innovations in Teaching and Learning Luncheon. We invited faculty colleagues to participate in the project with an eye towards capturing a range of learning environments, disciplines, students, and instructors" (document emailed to authors, September 1, 2019).

- Stacey Lawrence, senior associate director for STEM initiatives, and Mary Wright, associate provost for teaching and learning and executive director, in the Harriet W. Sheridan Center for Teaching and Learning at Brown University: "Although the Sheridan Center had been in existence for over 40 years, we were a relatively new integrated center bridging teaching initiatives and learning support with a number of new programs to fill Brown's strategic plan for teaching and learning. During Martin's visit, we focused on Sheridan programs and staff as part of this transition" (document emailed to authors, August 21. 2019).

- Serge Petchenyi, multimedia creative lead, Diane Sempler, senior associate director, and Mathew Ouellett, executive director in the Center for Teaching Excellence, Cornell University: "Having recently merged academic technologies and teaching center units, *The Teaching and Learning Project* provided an entirely new way to think about photography and the work of the media team in our newly combined center" (document emailed to authors, September 1, 2019).

Reflections from these contributors explore several aspects of change in the sections that follow: changing communication, changing community, and changing practice.

Changing Communication

Images are a common element in post-secondary institutional communications; photographs regularly occupy prominent places in college and university magazines, admissions brochures, websites, digital materials, and displays on walls and in hallways within physical spaces. Campuses participating in *The Teaching and Learning Project* approached this work with the hopes of improving communication and ended up with valuable new resources to enhance digital and print materials. At the University of Michigan, for example, Collette explained that "the photographs have been a key resource in publicity and communication about our services, programs, and events. They've been utilized in our annual reports, blog posts, project presentations and brochures, and are a prominent feature on the inaugural website of the new University of Michigan-led multi-institution Sloan Equity and Inclusion in STEM Introductory Courses research initiative." But the nature of these photographs provided more than utility: Martin's work,

7.02
A page spread from Caltech's Engineering & Science magazine features The Teaching and Learning Project photographs to illustrate the doctoral institution's commitment to teaching and learning. (Photograph reprinted with permission from the institution, courtesy of Caltech Magazine).

in the tradition of documentary photography, differs from images geared toward advertising; it also draws upon his experience as a postsecondary instructor and educational developer. As such, these photographs helped campuses change the nature of communications about teaching and learning. At Caltech, Martin visited and made photographs soon after the launch of the new teaching center. The resulting images were compelling, showing modern classes rather than staged interactions, and they captured institution-wide attention. This momentum helped spur the publication of a prominent article on new teaching-related initiatives in the campus's flagship publication, spreading awareness of and interest in improving teaching (Allan 2013). The photographs also served as artwork for the center's physical space, surrounding center visitors with meaningful, compelling images.

Participants at Wayne State University experienced similar impacts on communication about teaching and learning:

The images from the project changed the way we used visuals to articulate and communicate our priorities. We placed posters of our faculty and staff everywhere, especially in the library and classroom spaces. The images were quickly incorporated into our website and print publications, becoming central to all of our communications with faculty. Once others saw these photos, they intuitively understood their power to authentically communicate the teaching and learning experience, hence the provost's office and student support offices wanted to use these photos, as opposed to staged or stock photos.

Other project participants found new and vital ways to represent their own work. Lawrence and Wright at Brown University observed:

Like many educational developers, we have facilitated numerous workshops and receive feedback from instructors about the sense of community and support they experience in our programs. However, prior to Martin's visit, we did not have access to photos that represent this sentiment. In fact, when putting together reports or promotional materials, it is relatively difficult to capture the essence of our work. The typical images are usually posed group photos at events and institutes. Occasionally, we have candid photos of awardees, but not of the moments that preceded their awards. We cannot convey the work we do with static images because educational development is dynamic, just as teaching is dynamic.

Lawrence and Wright invite us to revisit a theme explored in chapter 2, emotion. They have encountered "a stereotypical view of center for teaching and learning spaces as locations of remediation." What they found in Martin's photographs, though, was a palpable sense of joy, which became an important lever for change:

An aspect of the Sheridan Center's work that is made visible through the photographs is the enthusiasm that participants bring to our programs. Many of the images highlight a sense of vibrancy and joy, whether it is a highly animated graduate student in a Sheridan program or a faculty member who is laughing together with students. As a tool to make joy visible, *The Teaching and Learning Project* photographs serve as a powerful lever to motivate other instructors to engage in instructional development. In our annual reports or work with our development office, we frequently pull from these photos because of their power in capturing this essence of our work.

7.03–7.04
Sequence of two photographs: Staff in a center for teaching and learning at a doctoral institution conduct a session for faculty and graduate students during a teaching certificate program.

7.05–7.07
Sequence of three photographs: Faculty and graduate students at a doctoral institution engage in discussion during a teaching certificate program at a center for teaching and learning.

7.08–7.10
Sequence of three photographs: A staff member in a center for teaching and learning at a doctoral institution facilitates a session for faculty and graduate students during a teaching certificate program.

Changing Community

Campuses also employed photographs—and even the process of deciding what, where, and whom to photograph—in creative ways, leading to enriching community interactions, deeper relationships, connections across institutional silos, and a profound sense of recognition that is often missing in the day-to-day work of postsecondary instructors.

Institutions have employed a variety of approaches to selecting classes and locations for Martin to visit and make photographs, including open calls for participants, invitations related to a particular theme such as large classes, or selection based on breadth of subjects and locations included in the photographs. View the online resource "Sample Institutional Visit Schedules" to see examples of what such schedules have included. Regardless of the process, participants found that the act of documentary photography itself opened up new pathways for acknowledging the value, effort, and importance of teaching, as Hood explains for Penn State University: "When our teaching center invited Martin, we reasoned that having photos would make teaching more visible to the university community. But we also learned in the process that the very act of taking a photo made teaching more valuable. To take a photo of someone's actions emphasizes the importance of those actions. Asking faculty for permission to take photos communicates that they and their actions are worth documenting; it communicates respect for the work they do as teachers." Kacin and Ouellett expand on that sense of valuing the work of teaching in especially challenging times:

> Like many public research universities, Wayne State University has experienced significant cuts in state support over the past decade. While good teaching is certainly important, other aspects of the faculty role are weighted differently, such as building one's research profile. There was little recent history of celebrating teaching and

learning as a campus community, although there were certainly exceptions at the department and college levels. After Martin's visit, everybody wanted copies of their classroom photos. For many, it was the first time seeing themselves in the act of teaching. It has been really lovely to see faculty recognize the significance of their work as teachers in new ways through this project.

Similarly, the work of those who support teaching and learning on campuses can often seem invisible or misunderstood. Oversimplified representations of academic staff roles in higher education abound; sometimes, they are even vilified or portrayed as requiring no particular expertise, despite the often-extensive academic and professional preparation needed to effectively work in such roles (Bessette 2021). Educational developers, a subset of academic staff who tend to bring a particularly wide range of disciplinary backgrounds and experiences to their work (Green and Little 2016), have at times struggled with a sense of precariousness (Sutherland 2015), which contradicts their positive ability to effect change (Plank 2019). *The Teaching and Learning Project* brought a new sense of recognition and clarity to these roles, as Lawrence and Wright discuss with respect to their own work: "We found that Martin's lens made visible our work and highlighted a key lever for change, enjoyment. We would encourage other campuses to consider how they might use images to not only raise the visibility of teaching through photos of campus instructors, but also to leverage the core values engaged in their own work, such as reflection and enjoyment, through photos of themselves."

Several institutions organized exhibits of photographs and other events in connection with their participation in *The Teaching and Learning Project*; examples of these exhibit materials are also available in the online resource "Photographic Exhibits in Higher Education: Examples and Suggestions." Exhibits in which campus communities had the chance to see and reflect on their educational endeavors have become unexpectedly meaningful experiences. At Wayne State University, Kacin and Ouellett "blew up the photos to poster size and curated an exhibit in the atrium of our Undergraduate Library. With students, faculty, and staff moving through this building on a daily basis, it is an essential hub on campus. Students loved seeing themselves and their instructors to the point that some posters even 'walked off.'" At Cornell University, the resulting exhibit focused on particular teaching strategies, leading to deeper engagement and connection:

> The spring 2019 provost's seminar on teaching and learning was the first time we presented a public exhibition of the digital prints highlighting the active learning strategies happening in our classrooms. The photos were set up on easels along the perimeter of the reception area. As people walked into the room, they saw their colleagues and friends caught in the act of teaching. Instead of proceeding into the main dining room, everyone stopped, clustered around the posters, and talked to each other. In a moment, people were able to see and think in a different way, to be attentive to details, and, through the images, pierce the veil of isolation that can surround teaching.

The very act of coming together to look at photographs can serve as a catalyst for interaction and recognition. Penn State University tapped into this potential with a gala event featuring *The Teaching and Learning Project* photographs, attended by faculty and campus leaders; instructors helped select images and stood next to their photographs during the event: "Some faculty appeared pleasantly overwhelmed by the experience, which gave them a chance to talk about their work with others, including those responsible for making decisions about teaching at the university. Upper-level administrators seemed to come away with a better sense of what happens in classes every day across the university." Caltech also created an exhibit featuring images from *The Teaching and Learning Project* along with photographs made by students and staff and archival images from the institution's history; it was located in a common area that serves as the main entrance to the teaching center and where students, faculty, and staff often gather before and after meetings and events. This exhibit, "Teaching and Writing at Caltech: Past, Present, Future" was a collaboration between the teaching center, writing center, and university archives; its creation extended our shared commitments to the intentional use of visual rhetoric and engaged the campus and alumni community (Caltech 2018).

Such events can play a significant role in bridging divides between institutional roles and creating a more positive campus climate. For example, Huelsbeck discusses new insights at Rochester Community and Technical College, one of thirty-seven campuses in the Minnesota State system:

> I have often felt that I am an outsider in regards to the system-wide efforts. My colleagues are inclined to vent their frustrations with the system's requirements. Many faculty seem to perceive that we are given so many hurdles that aren't relevant to our day-to-day job of teaching our students. *The Teaching and Learning Project* exhibition helped to present the system of teaching and learning in a different light. It was a revelation to me that an artist, dedicated to improving teaching and learning, would be able to create work in this vein without irony—that in fact an artist would make work that, while realistic in its portrayal of the everyday mundane aspect of the work of teaching and learning, in the end could discover the nobility and the purpose of the work that we do each and every day.

These examples showcase the power of photographs, especially when viewed and discussed in community, to spark deeper understanding between and across people, roles, and organizational units within postsecondary institutions.

7.11–7.12
Sequence of two photographs: Faculty, administrators, and staff view and reflect on prints from The Teaching and Learning Project made at their institutions. (Reproduced by permission from Deidre Yingling.)

7.13–7.14
Sequence of two photographs: Students at an associate's institution view photographs from The Teaching and Learning Project made at their institution. (Reproduced by permission from Luke Austin.)

Changing Practice

An unexpected yet powerful use of the photographs from *The Teaching and Learning Project* builds on the communication and community impacts described above, but brings the photographs into formal professional development for postsecondary instructors and into the larger context of organizational change. At the University of Michigan, educational developers found the photos to be "immensely valuable in icebreaker activities and as prompts for reflection and group discussion. In course design sessions, the images are a great vantage point from which participants can observe the complex ecosystem of large courses. They have generated rich discussions about inclusive teaching, climate, and student experience in foundational courses, and about visible labor and the more behind-the-scenes work of teaching and managing them. They also helped build empathy across roles about the reality for various course stakeholders." Collette further explains how and why this might be the case:

> The photographs have enhanced audience rapport and participation. Attendees at our events hold various roles on campus (administrative leaders, faculty, lecturers, graduate student instructors, undergraduate instructors) and come from a variety of academic disciplines. As facilitators, we strive to create structures for effective brainstorming and collaboration, encouraging participants to learn from each other. However, with different identities, life experiences, and power hierarchies, inaccurate and hurtful preconceived notions, as well as feelings of hesitation, vulnerability, and impatience across roles, can surface. When we've used *The Teaching and Learning Project* images as facilitation tools, participants tend to more easily offer their thoughts and experiences, and are willing to strategize together about improvements to classroom practices. We hypoth-

esize that the photographs provide a useful distance from personal experience and in this neutral zone of engagement, barriers in the room, perceived and real, are more readily lowered.

Penn State University has also incorporated photographs into their professional development programming. The images allow facilitators to ask specific questions, which engage participants and draw them into reflections on teaching, for example: "What do you notice about the body language of the instructor and/or students? What is the instructor doing to make contact with the students? What is happening in this class? What do you see that makes you say that?" Participants' answers lead to further investigation:

> The responses show not only what people think teaching is, but what they see as their own teaching challenges. Frequently viewers notice that in one particular photo, students' heads are turned in different directions. When asked why they are interpreting the photo as evidence of success or failure, people begin to support their impressions by pointing out details: some students are writing in their notebooks, so they must be paying attention. Other students have laptops open, so they must not be paying attention. These observations provide pathway to a discussion of how teachers interpret student actions and enable participants to identify alternate interpretations. A photo can offer teachers the opportunity to identify what they expect of students and brainstorm ways to more explicitly communicate their expectations.

We encourage you to use this book and its supplementary resources and guides, all made available under a Creative Commons license (https://CreativeCommons.org/licenses/by-nc-nd/4.0), for professional development at your institution. In particular, the "Close Reading and Observation Exercises," available at https://www.CenterForEngagedLearning.org/books/what-teaching-looks-like, include selections that portray complex and thought-provoking teaching environments and interactions, and have the potential, through reflection and facilitated discussion, to spark dialogue and insights among instructors, staff, administrators, and others.

At Cornell University, engagement with *The Teaching and Learning Project* also served an internal professional development purpose, supporting staff members from media production and academic backgrounds who had recently merged into a new center, to share experiences and establish common ground. For those with media expertise, joining photoshoots and discussing photographs "helped the team transition from a production unit to one with a pedagogical approach." Following Martin's visit, this team continued to make photographs focusing on active learning in real classrooms. They also adapted the consultation process developed for use with faculty (Springborg and Horii 2016) for conversations among media and academic staff, resulting in "a deeply enriching internal professional development opportunity for our team. In our own unit, we are now more aware of what our work is. Through photography, we are developing our ability to observe, listen, and engage in meaningful conversations with each other."

Some campuses have intentionally brought *The Teaching and Learning Project* photographs to bear on larger goals and challenges as a change practice and as part of a coherent change strategy. For example, the University of Michigan foundational course initiative was aiming for large-scale changes, and the photographs helped them establish a baseline from which to measure such change: "Martin observed and photographed twenty distinct teaching and learning spaces, including large lecture auditoriums, small discussion sections, labs, office hours, peer-led study groups and writing consultations, exam halls, and instructional team meetings. Our three-day agenda enabled documentation of the multifaceted student-student, instructor-student, and instructor-instructor interactions that are typical in these mammoth operations." Whereas people at the University of Michigan sought a more thorough understanding of a particular kind of teaching and learning environment, at Caltech they helped remedy a mismatch between reality and shared conceptions. Getting Martin into real classes helped to change and expand the institution's shared conceptual model of teaching. It may be a cliché, but being able to show today's teaching environment to varied campus stakeholders through photographs was worth many thousands of words.

Others have built photography into their organizational change strategies. At Wayne State University, "as a part of making teaching a more public and dynamic aspect of campus life, *The Teaching and Learning Project* made a discernable and important impact on warming up the climate for talking about teaching and learning in a kinder, friendlier way. The outgrowths of this program led to other complementary initiatives, too, such as our burgeoning Thank-a-Teacher program and the faculty-led Wayne State University Academy of Teachers." At Brown University, the photographs contributed to a shared identity among Sheridan Center staff as leaders of organizational change: "We are located in a library, and having photos of our work in action gives passersby a glimpse of what happens in a workshop, class, small-group consultation, or tutoring session. They make our work visible. As facilitators, these photos have prompted our reflection on the work of Sheridan Center staff and capture how we are agents of change on our own campuses." This self-recognition is an empowering form of support for academic staff doing transformational, but sometimes invisible, work to improve teaching and learning.

7.15
The Teaching and Learning Project photographs on permanent display in a center for teaching and learning at a doctoral institution. (Reproduced by permission from Ching Lee.)

7.16

Staff in a center for teaching and learning at a doctoral institution prepare prints from The Teaching and Learning Project for display during an annual teaching and learning summit. (Reproduced by permission from the University of Virginia Center for Teaching Excellence.)

Making Photographs in Your Context

At this point, we hope you are excited about the possibility of incorporating authentic, documentary-style photographs into your efforts to change and improve communication, community, and educational practice within your own context. In addition to those already mentioned elsewhere, the online resources associated with this volume, available at https://www.CenterForEngagedLearning. org/books/what-teaching-looks-like, include samples of the following often-requested artifacts and materials. We find that when starting to make photographs of postsecondary teaching and learning, these examples support those efforts, even as you may need to adapt the exact language and formats for your institution:

- "Guide to Making Photographs in Higher Education"—A short guide to making photographs of teaching and learning in a documentary style within higher education institutions, including working with professional photographers and those in training.
- "Sample Photograph Release Form" for subjects appearing in photographs.
- "Close Reading and Observation Exercises"—Prompts to use with specific photographs and sequences of photographs for use in reflection and discussion on educational practices (e.g., one-on-one and in educational/ professional development programs).
- "Photography-Based Instructional Consultation Prompts"—A guide to using photographs as part of individual consultations on teaching, particularly with the same instructors whose classes appear in the images.

In addition, we refer you to the discussion and references in the introduction to this volume related to creating long-form descriptive text to accompany photographs, so that your use of images may be as accessible as possible for members of your community.

Future Roles of Photographs

Beyond supporting positive change within institutions, we believe that photographs have as-yet-unimagined roles to play in contributing to and shaping modern narratives about higher education. With new urgency, images like these have a place in building public trust, communicating the purposes and potentials of postsecondary education, and in advancing the sense of belonging and inclusion for diverse students, faculty, and staff. They also hold the promise of helping the higher education community grapple with its shortcomings and move forward collectively, with both intellectual and affective commitment, through the new ways of seeing that photographs make possible.

The recognition of the power of images is growing within institutions of higher education. We have started to see postsecondary organizations embracing the metaphor of thinking through images, as with the Association of American Colleges and Universities effort to better define and communicate "What Liberal Education Looks Like" (AAC&U 2020). Viji Sathy, a teaching professor of psychology and neuroscience at the University of North Carolina at Chapel Hill, brings her photographic practice into classrooms, focusing on "visual representations of inclusiveness in educational spaces" (Sathy, n.d.). A growing number of faculty across disciplines, not only in the arts, are harnessing the power of photographs, both to enhance and reflect on their teaching practices. And with those photographs come new discussions with communications professionals about the ways in which authentic images can support institutional missions and goals.

Building on these new directions, we hope that postsecondary teachers, staff, administrators, and students are left with a sense of empowerment. Whether you endeavor to make photographs yourself, collaborate with students and faculty in a nearby art department, or use this volume and accompanying online resources to launch professional learning communities exploring photography in higher education, the images you make about your own educational context and experiences will have the potential to open up new conversations and collaborations within and beyond your institutions. May our understanding of what teaching looks like continue to evolve alongside our educational practices, with and through photographs that reflect the beauty and complexity of higher education.

7.17
A classroom at a doctoral institution is empty, quiet, and ready for students to arrive.

REFERENCES

AAC&U (Association of American Colleges and Universities). 2020. "What Liberal Education Looks Like: What It Is, Who It's For, & Where It Happens." https://portal.criticalimpact.com/user/25043/image/whatlibedlookslike. pdf.

AAUP (American Association of University Professors). 2018. "Data Snapshot: Contingent Faculty in US Higher Ed." October 11, 2018. https://www. aaup.org/news/data-snapshot-contingent-faculty-us-higher-ed.

ACE (American Council on Education). 2021. "Women's Representation in Higher Education Leadership Around the World." International Briefs for Higher Education Leaders, No 9. https://www.acenet.edu/Research-Insights/Pages/Internationalization/International-Briefs-for-Higher-Education-Leaders.aspx.

Agee, James, and Walker Evans. 1960. *Let Us Now Praise Famous Men.* Boston: Houghton Mifflin Company.

Allan, Andrew. 2013. "Evolving Education." *Engineering and Science* 76 (3): 28–31. https://resolver.caltech.edu/CaltechES:20170811-101023219.

Ambrose, Susan, Michael W. Bridges, Michele DiPietro, Marsha C. Lovett, and Marie K. Norman. 2010. *How Learning Works: Seven Research-Based Principles for Smart Teaching.* San Francisco: Jossey-Bass.

American Academy of Arts & Sciences. 2017. "The Future of Undergraduate Education: The Future of America." Commission on the Future of Undergraduate Education. https://www.amacad.org/publication/future-undergraduate-education.

Arum, Richard, and Josipa Roksa. 2011. *Academically Adrift: Limited Learning on College Campuses.* Chicago: University of Chicago Press.

ASCN (Accelerating Systemic Change in STEM Higher Education). n.d. "About ASCN." Accessed December 7, 2020. https://ascnhighered.org/ASCN/about.html.

Astin, Alexander W. 2016. *Are You Smart Enough? How Colleges' Obsession with Smartness Shortchanges Students.* Sterling, VA: Stylus Publishing, LLC.

Baker, Lane A., Devasmita Chakraverty, Linda Columbus, Andrew L. Feig, William S. Jenks, Matthew Pilarz, Marilyne Stains, Rory Waterman, and Jodi L. Wesemann. 2014. "Cottrell Scholars Collaborative New Faculty Workshop: Professional Development for New Chemistry Faculty and Initial Assessment of Its Efficacy." *Journal of Chemical Education* 91, no. 11 (November 11): 1874–81. https://doi.org/10.1021/ed500547n.

Bard Microcollege. n.d. Accessed December 26, 2020. https://microcollege.bard.edu/.

Baron-Nixon, Leora. 2007. *Connecting Non Full-time Faculty to Institutional Mission: A Guidebook for College/University Administrators and Faculty Developers.* Sterling, VA: Stylus Publishing, LLC.

Barr, Robert, and John Tagg. 1995. "From Teaching to Learning—A New Paradigm for Undergraduate Education." *Change: The Magazine of Higher Learning* 27, no. 6 (November 1): 12–26. https://doi.org/10.1080/00091383.1995.10544672.

Bates, A. W. (Tony). 2019. *Teaching in a Digital Age: Guidelines for Designing Teaching and Learning.* British Columbia: BC Open Textbooks. https://opentextbc.ca/teachinginadigitalage/.

Beghetto, Ronald A. 2019. *Beautiful Risks: Having the Courage to Teach and Learn Creatively.* Lanham, MD: Rowman & Littlefield.

Berger, John. 2013. *Understanding a Photograph.* Ed. Geoff Dyer. London: Penguin Books.

Bessette, Lee Skallerup. 2020. "Advice: Staff Get Little to No Say in Campus Governance. That Must Change." *Chronicle of Higher Education*, September 22, 2020. https://www.chronicle.com/article/staff-get-little-to-no-say-in-campus-governance-that-must-change.

Bessette, Lee Skallerup. 2021. "Stop Ignoring Microaggressions Against Your Staff." *Chronicle of Higher Education*, March 8, 2021. https://www.chronicle.com/article/stop-ignoring-microaggressions-against-your-staff.

Bey, Dawoud. 2018. "Class Pictures." In *Seeing Deeply,* 192–247. Austin: University of Texas Press.

Bjork, Robert A. 1994. "Memory and Metamemory Considerations in the Training of Human Beings." In *Metacognition: Knowing about Knowing*, edited by J. Metcalfe and A. Shimamura, 185–205. Cambridge: MIT Press.

Blouin, David D., and Evelyn M. Perry. 2009. "Whom Does Service Learning Really Serve? Community-Based Organizations' Perspectives on Service Learning." *Teaching Sociology* 37, no. 2 (April): 120–35. https://doi.org/10.1177/0092055X0903700201.

Bok, Derek. 2017. *The Struggle to Reform Our Colleges.* Princeton: Princeton University Press.

Border, Laura L. B., ed. 2011. *Mapping the Range of Graduate Student Professional Development*. Stillwater, OK: New Forums Press.

Boyer, Ernest L. 1990. "Scholarship Reconsidered: Priorities of the Professoriate." Special Report, December 3, 1990. Carnegie Foundation for the Advancement of Teaching. https://files.eric.ed.gov/fulltext/ED326149.pdf.

Boys, Jos. 2011. *Towards Creative Learning Spaces: Rethinking the Architecture of Post-Compulsory Education.* New York: Routledge.

Brail, Shauna. 2013. "Experiencing the City: Urban Studies Students and Service Learning." *Journal of Geography in Higher Education* 37, no. 2 (May 1): 241–56. https://doi.org/10.1080/03098265.2012.763115.

Brookfield, Stephen. 1995. *Becoming a Critically Reflective Teacher.* San Francisco: Jossey-Bass.

Brookfield, Stephen. 2019. "Teaching for Critical Thinking." Workshop at Indiana University East, August 21, 2019. http://www.stephenbrookfield.com/powerpoints-pdfs.

Bruff, Derek. 2018. "Active Learning Classrooms: What We Know." *Agile Learning: Derek Bruff's Blog on Teaching and Technology,* September 11, 2018. https://derekbruff.org/?p=3363.

Bruff, Derek. 2019. *Intentional Tech.* Morgantown, VA: West Virginia University Press.

Burns, Sean, and Mark McCormack. 2020. "Evidence of a New Normal: Surveys on Online Services and Courses." Educause, September 15, 2020. https://www.educause.edu/ecar/research-publications/fall-planning-for-the-new-normal-moving-higher-ed-online/evidence-of-a-new-normal-surveys-on-online-services-and-courses.

Busman, Debra. 2017. "Silences and Stories: Honoring Voice and Agency in the College Classroom." In *Ways of Being in Teaching: Conversations and Reflections,* edited by Sean Wiebe, Ellyn Lyle, Peter R. Wright, Kimberly Dark, Mitchell McLarnon, and Liz Day, 47–54. Rotterdam: Sense Publishers.

Butrymowicz, Sarah, and Pete D'Amato. 2020. "A Crisis is Looming for U.S. Colleges—and Not Just Because of the Pandemic." *The Hechinger Report,* August 4, 2020. https://www.nbcnews.com/news/education/crisis-looming-u-s-colleges-not-just-because-pandemic-n1235338.

Caldwell-O'Keefe, Riley, and Matt Recla. 2020. "'Slowly Changing the World': Embedding Experiential Learning to Enhance Ethics and Diversity." In *Integrating Community Service into the Curriculum: International Perspectives on Humanizing Higher Education*, edited by Enakshi Sengupta, Patrick Blessenger, and Mandla Makhanya, 147–64. *Innovations in Higher Education Teaching and Learning* 25. Bingley: Emerald Publishing Limited. https://doi.org/10.1108/S2055-364120200000025010.

Caltech. 2018. "Teaching and Writing at Caltech: Past, Present, Future." Center for Teaching, Learning & Outreach, Exhibit website, April 23-27, 2018. http://ctlo.caltech.edu/universityteaching/events/teachweek/teachweek2018/exhibit2018.

Caltech Archives. 2017. "Celebrating the New Academic Year." Posted September 26, 2017. Online exhibit. https://archives.caltech.edu/exhibits/students_60s/.

Caltech Archives. 2021. "Classroom." Image search. https://digital.archives.caltech.edu/islandora/search/classroom?type=edismax&cp=caltech%3Aimages.

Campus Compact. n.d. "Who We Are." Accessed November 25, 2020. https://compact.org/who-we-are/.

Caponigro, John. 1998. "An Interview with Emmet Gowin (1998). Posted on September 22, 2010, by Editorial @ ASX. https://americansuburbx.com/2010/09/theory-interview-with-emmet-gowin.html.

Carnegie (Carnegie Classification of Institutions of Higher Education). 2018. "Basic Classification Description." https://carnegieclassifications.iu.edu/classification_descriptions/basic.php.

Carnevale, Anthony P., and Jeff Strohl. 2013. "Separate & Unequal: How Higher Education Reinforces the Intergenerational Reproduction of White Racial Privilege." Georgetown University Center on Education and the Workforce, July 2013. https://cew.georgetown.edu/cew-reports/separate-unequal/.

Cook-Sather, Alison, Catherine Bovill, and Peter Felten. 2014. *Engaging Students as Partners in Learning and Teaching.* San Francisco: Jossey-Bass.

Cooper Hewitt. n.d. "Cooper Hewitt Guidelines for Image Description." Accessed October 30, 2021. https://www.cooperhewitt.org/cooper-hewitt-guidelines-for-image-description.

Cruz, Laura, Karen Huxtable-Jester, Brian Smentkowski, and Martin Springborg. 2021. "Place-based Educational Development: What Center for Teaching and Learning Spaces Look Like (and Why That Matters)." *To Improve the Academy* 40 (1): 75–104. https://doi.org/10.3998/tia.960.

Dark, Kimberly. 2017. "Education, Reaching." In *Ways of Being in Teaching: Conversations and Reflections*, edited by Sean Wiebe, Ellyn Lyle, Peter R. Wright, Kimberly Dark, Mitchell McLarnon, and Liz Day, 25–32. Rotterdam: Sense Publishers.

DeVaney, James. 2020. "Higher Ed Needs a Long-Term Plan for Virtual Learning." *Harvard Business Review*, May 5, 2020. https://hbr.org/2020/05/higher-ed-needs-a-long-term-plan-for-virtual-learning.

Diagram Center. n.d. "Image Description Guidelines." Accessed October 30, 2021. http://diagramcenter.org/table-of-contents-2.html.

Doorley, Scott, and Scott Witthoft. 2012. *Make Space: How to Set the Stage for Creative Collaboration.* Hoboken: John Wiley & Sons, Inc.

Douglas-Gabriel, Danielle. 2019. "'It Keeps You Nice and Disposable': The Plight of Adjunct Professors." *The Washington Post*, February 14, 2019. https://www.washingtonpost.com/local/education/it-keeps-you-nice-and-disposable-the-plight-of-adjunct-professors/2019/02/14/6cd5cbe4-024d-11e9-b5df-5d3874f1ac36_story.html.

Eagan, Kevin, Ellen Bara Stolzenberg, Jennifer Berdan Lozano, Melissa C. Aragon, Maria Ramirez Suchard, and Sylvia Hurtado. 2014. "Undergraduate Teaching Faculty: The 2013–2014 HERI Faculty Survey." Los Angeles: Higher Education Research Institute, UCLA. https://heri.ucla.edu/monographs/HERI-FAC2014-monograph.pdf.

Education Dive. 2020. "A Look at Trends in College Consolidation Since 2016." *Higher Ed Dive*, Updated September 17, 2020. https://www.highereddive.com/news/how-many-colleges-and-universities-have-closed-since-2016/539379/.

Estrada, Mica, Alegra Eroy-Reveles, and John Matsui. 2018. "The Influence of Affirming Kindness and Community on Broadening Participation in STEM Career Pathways," *Social Issues and Policy Review* 12, no. 1 (January): 258–97. https://doi.org/10.1111/sipr.12046.

Ewald, Wendy; coauthored by Alexandra Lightfoot. 2001. *I Wanna Take Me a Picture: Teaching Photography and Writing to Children*. Boston: Beacon Press.

Fain, Paul. 2019. "Study on Prison-Based College Programs." *Inside Higher Ed*, May 22, 2019. https://www.insidehighered.com/quicktakes/2019/05/22/study-prison-based-college-program.

Felten, Peter, Alan Kalish, Allison Pingree, and Kathryn M. Plank. 2007. "Toward a Scholarship of Teaching and Learning in Educational Development." *To Improve the Academy: A Journal of Educational Development* 25 (1): 93–108. http://dx.doi.org/10.3998/tia.17063888.0025.010.

Fossland, Trine, and Regnhild Sandvoll. 2021. "Drivers for Educational Change? Educational Leaders' Perceptions of Academic Developers as Change Agents. *International Journal for Academic Development,* June 17, 2021. https://doi.org/10.1080/1360144X.2021.1941034.

Freeman, Scott, Sarah L. Eddy, Miles McDonough, Michelle K. Smith, Nnadozie Okoroafor, Hannah Jordt, and Mary Pat Wenderoth. 2014. "Active Learning Increases Student Performance in Science, Engineering, and Mathematics." *Proceedings of the National Academy of Sciences* 111, no. 23 (June 10): 8410–15. https://doi.org/10.1073/pnas.1319030111.

Freire, Paulo. 1993. *Pedagogy of the Oppressed*. Translated by Myra Bergman Ramos. New York: Continuum Publishing Company.

Gachago, Daniela, Laura Cruz, Cheryl Belford, Candice Livingston, Jolanda Morkel, Sweta Patnaik, and Bronwyn Swartz. 2021. "Third Places: Cultivating Mobile Communities of Practice in the Global South." *International Journal for Academic Development*, July 26, 2021. https://doi.org/10.1080/1360144X.2021.1955363.

Geertsema, Johan, and Roeland van der Rijst. 2021. "Access and Success: Rethinking and Widening the Impact of Academic Development." *International Journal for Academic Development* 26 (1): 1-6. https://doi.org/10.1080/1360144X.2021.1876337.

Geertz, Clifford. 1973. "Thick Description: Toward an Interpretive Theory of Culture." In *Selected Essays by Clifford Geertz*, 3–30. New York: Basic Books.

Gerstmann, Evan. 2019. "How College in Prison Turns Around Lives and Saves Taxpayers Money." *Forbes*, November 23, 2019. https://www.forbes.com/sites/evangerstmann/2019/11/23/how-college-in-prison-turns-around-lives-and-saves-taxpayers-money/.

Gibbs, Graham. 2013. "Reflections on the Changing Nature of Educational Development." *International Journal for Academic Development* 18 (1): 4–14. https://doi.org/10.1080/1360144X.2013.751691.

Gibbs, Graham, and Martin Coffey. 2004. "The Impact of Training of University Teachers on Their Teaching Skills, Their Approach to Teaching and the Approach to Learning of Their Students." *Active Learning in Higher Education* 5 (1): 87–100. https://doi.org/10.1177/1469787404040463.

Green, David, and Deandra Little. 2016. "Family Portrait: A Profile of Educational Developers Around the World." *International Journal for Academic Development* 21 (2): 135–50. https://doi.org/10.1080/1360144X.2015.1046875.

Hart Research Associates. 2018. "Fulfilling the American Dream: Liberal Education and the Future of Work." Washington, DC: Association of American Colleges and Universities. https://www.aacu.org/research/2018-future-of-work.

Harvey, Marina. 2017. "Quality Learning and Teaching with Sessional Staff: Systematising Good Practice for Academic Development." *International Journal for Academic Development* 22 (1): 1–6. https://doi.org/10.1080/136014 4X.2017.1266753.

Henderson, Charles, Andrea Beach, and Noah Finkelstein. 2011. "Facilitating Change in Undergraduate STEM Instructional Practices: An Analytic Review of the Literature." *Journal of Research in Science Teaching* 48 (8): 952–84. https://doi.org/10.1002/tea.20439.

Henderson, Charles, Mark Connolly, Erin L. Dolan, Noah Finkelstein, Scott Franklin, Shirley Malcom, Chris Rasmussen, Kacy Redd, and Kristen St. John. 2017. "Towards the STEM DBER Alliance: Why We Need a Discipline-Based STEM Education Research Community." *International Journal of Research in Undergraduate Mathematics Education* 3, no. 2 (July 1): 247–54. https://doi.org/10.1007/s40753-017-0056-3.

Hess, Abigail. 2020. "How Coronavirus Dramatically Changed College for over 14 Million Students." CNBC, March 26, 2020. https://www.cnbc.com/2020/03/26/how-coronavirus-changed-college-for-over-14-million-students.html.

Hill, Lucas B., Julia N. Savoy, Ann E. Austin, and Bipana Bantawa. 2019. "The Impact of Multi-Institutional STEM Reform Networks on Member Institutions: A Case Study of CIRTL." *Innovative Higher Education* 44, no. 3 (June 1): 187–202. https://doi.org/10.1007/s10755-019-9461-7.

hooks, bell. 1994. *Teaching to Transgress: Education as the Practice of Freedom*. New York: Routledge.

Hoover, Elona, and Marie K. Harder. 2015. "What Lies beneath the Surface? The Hidden Complexities of Organizational Change for Sustainability in Higher Education." *Journal of Cleaner Production* 106 (1 November 2015): 175–88. http://dx.doi.org/10.1016/j.jclepro.2014.01.081.

Horii, Cassandra, and Mitch Aiken. 2013. "STEM Outreach as Integrative Learning: Enhancing K-12 STEM Pathways for Underserved Schools." Poster presented at the Association of American Colleges & Universities Transforming STEM Education Conference, October 31 – November 2, 2013. San Diego, CA.

Hostetler, Lisa. 2004. "The New Documentary Tradition in Photography." In Heilbrunn Timeline of Art History. New York: The Metropolitan Museum of Art. http://www.metmuseum.org/toah/hd/ndoc/hd_ndoc.htm.

House Committee on Education and the Workforce. 2014. "The Just-In-Time Professor: A Staff Report Summarizing eForum Responses on the Working Conditions of Contingent Faculty in Higher Education." US House of Representatives, January 2014. https://edlabor.house.gov/imo/media/doc/1.24.14-AdjunctEforumReport.pdf.

Hunt, Brian, Rick Eskil, James Blethen and Alasdair Stewart. 2019. "Community Colleges Can't Be Ignored in State Budget." *Walla Walla Union-Bulletin*, April 21, 2019. https://www.union-bulletin.com/opinion/editorials/community-colleges-can-t-be-ignored-in-state-budget/article_eb0e1ea4-62c8-11e9-bd2d-3fc3be97f65f.html.

Hunter, Anna. 2020. "Snapshots of Selfhood: Curating Academic Identity through Visual Autoethnography." *International Journal for Academic Development* 25 (4): 310–23. https://doi.org/10.1080/1360144X.2020.1755865.

Hurtado, Sylvia, Kevin Eagan, John H. Pryor, Hannah Whang, and Serge Tran. 2012. "Undergraduate Teaching Faculty: The 2010–2011 HERI Faculty Survey." Los Angeles: Higher Education Research Institute, UCLA. https://www.heri.ucla.edu/monographs/HERI-FAC2011-Monograph.pdf.

Hussar, Bill, Jijun Zhang, Sarah Hein, Ke Wang, Ashley Roberts, Jiashan Cui, Mary Smith, Farrah Bullock Mann, Amy Barmer, and Rita Dilig; Thomas Nachazel, Megan Barnett, and Stephen Purcell, eds. 2020. *The Condition of Education 2020*. Washington, DC: National Center for Education Statistics. Publication #2020144. https://nces.ed.gov/pubs2020/2020144.pdf.

Hutchings, Pat, Mary Taylor Huber, and Anthony Ciccone. 2011. *The Scholarship of Teaching and Learning Reconsidered: Institutional Integration and Impact*. Hoboken: John Wiley & Sons.

Illeris, Knud. 2014. *Transformative Learning and Identity*. New York: Routledge.

Karasik, Rona J. 2020. "Community Partners' Perspectives and the Faculty Role in Community-Based Learning." *Journal of Experiential Education* 43, no. 2 (June): 113–35. https://doi.org/10.1177/1053825919892994.

Kelly, Rob. 2019. "Balancing the Demands of Teaching, Scholarship, and Service." Magna Publications, November 25. https://www.facultyfocus.com/articles/faculty-development/teaching-careers-balancing-the-demands-of-teaching-scholarship-and-service/.

"Ken Burns Presents: College Behind Bars." 2019. Directed by Lynn Novick. Arlington, VA: PBS.

Kendi, Ibram X. 2016. *Stamped from the Beginning: The Definitive History of Racist Ideas in America.* New York: Bold Type Books.

Kezar, Adrianna, Tom DePaola, and Daniel T. Scott. 2019. *The Gig Academy: Mapping Labor in the Neoliberal University.* Baltimore: Johns Hopkins University Press, 2019).

Kimie, Itakura. 2021. "The Tragedy of the Part-Time Lecturer: Poverty on the Rise Among Japan's PhDs." August 19, 2021, Nippon.com. https://www.nippon.com/en/in-depth/d00721/.

King, Alison. 1993. "From Sage on the Stage to Guide on the Side." *College Teaching* 41, no. 1 (Winter): 30–35.

Knaub, Alexis V., Kathleen T. Foote, Charles Henderson, Melissa Dancy, and Robert J. Beichner. 2016. "Get a Room: The Role of Classroom Space in Sustained Implementation of Studio Style Instruction." *International Journal of STEM Education* 3, no. 8. https://doi.org/https://doi.org/10.1186/s40594-016-0042-3.

Kuh, George D. 2008. *High-Impact Educational Practices: What They Are, Who Has Access to Them, and Why They Matter.* Washington, DC: Association of American Colleges and Universities.

Kumar, Ravi, and Dave Hill. 2009. "Neoliberal Capitalism and Education." In *Global Neoliberalism and Education and its Consequences*, edited by Dave Hill and Ravi Kumar, 1–11. New York: Routledge.

Lagemann, Ellen Condliffe. 2002. A*n Elusive Science: The Troubling History of Education Research.* Chicago: University of Chicago Press.

Lang, James M. 2018. "Do Photos of Teaching on Your Campus Look Staged and Static?" *The Chronicle of Higher Education,* May 22, 2018. https://www.chronicle.com/article/do-photos-of-teaching-on-your-campus-look-staged-and-static/.

Lange, Dorothea. 1964. Interviewed by Richard Doud, New York City, May 22, 1964. Archives of American Art, Smithsonian Institution. https://www.aaa.si.edu/collections/interviews/oral-history-interview-dorothea-lange-11757.

Lara, Miguel, and Kate Lockwood. 2016. "Hackathons as Community-Based Learning: A Case Study." *Techtrends* 60, no. 5 (September): 486–95. https://doi.org/10.1007/s11528-016-0101-0.

Laursen, Sandra. 2019. *Levers for Change: An Assessment of Progress on Changing STEM Instruction.* Washington, DC: American Association for the Advancement of Science. https://www.aaas.org/resources/levers-change-assessment-progress-changing-stem-instruction.

Lederman, Doug. 2019. "Professors' Slow, Steady Acceptance of Online Learning: A Survey." *Inside Higher Ed*, October 30, 2019. https://www.insidehighered.com/news/survey/professors-slow-steady-acceptance-online-learning-survey.

Lederman, Doug. 2020. "Faculty Confidence in Online Learning Grows." *Inside Higher Ed*, October 6, 2020. https://www.insidehighered.com/digital-learning/article/2020/10/06/covid-era-experience-strengthens-faculty-belief-value-online.

Levy, David C. 2012. "Do Professors Work Enough?" *The Washington Post*, March 24, 2012. https://www.washingtonpost.com/opinions/do-college-professors-work-hard-enough/2012/02/15/gIQAn058VS_story.html.

Little, Deandra, and David A. Green. 2012. "Betwixt and Between: Academic Developers in the Margins." *International Journal for Academic Development* 17 (3): 203–15. http://dx.doi.org/10.1080/1360144X.2012.700895.

Longmire-Avital, Buffie. 2018. "Seven Potential Barriers to Engaging in Undergraduate Research for HURMS." Center for Engaged Learning (blog), September 18, 2018. https://www.centerforengagedlearning.org/seven-potential-barriers-to-engaging-in-undergraduate-research-for-hurms/.

Longmire-Avital, Buffie. 2019a. "What's Their Capital? Applying a Community Cultural Wealth Model to UR." Center for Engaged Learning (blog), March 4, 2019. https://www.centerforengagedlearning.org/whats-their-capital-applying-a-community-cultural-wealth-model-to-ur/.

Longmire-Avital, Buffie. 2019b. "Tackling Inequitable Opportunity Structures in HIPs." Center for Engaged Learning (blog), July 16, 2019. https://www.centerforengagedlearning.org/tackling-inequitable-opportunity-structures-in-hips/.

Longmire-Avital, Buffie. 2020. "Critical Mentoring in HIPs: A Reparative Framework." Center for Engaged Learning (blog), July 2, 2020. https://www.centerforengagedlearning.org/Critical-Mentoring-in-HIPs-A-Reparative-Framework.

Malcom-Piqueux, Lindsey. 2020. "Transformation in the U.S. Higher Education System: Implications for Racial Equity." Symposium on Imagining the Future of Undergraduate STEM Education, Board on Science Education, National Academy of Sciences, Engineering, and Medicine. https://stemfutureshighered.secure-platform.com/a/page/Papers.

Marcus, Jon. 2016. "The Paradox of New Buildings on Campus." *The Atlantic*, July 25, 2016. https://www.theatlantic.com/education/archive/2016/07/the-paradox-of-new-buildings-on-campus/492398/.

Mather, Phillippe. 2013. *Stanley Kubrick at Look Magazine: Authorship and Genre in Photojournalism and Film*. Chicago: The University of Chicago Press.

McKenzie, Lindsay. 2019. "Changing Spaces." *Inside Higher Ed*, August 14, 2019. https://www.insidehighered.com/digital-learning/article/2019/08/14/changing-role-physical-campuses-online-education.

Morris, Willie. 1988. "The American Classroom." In *American Classroom: The Photographs of Catherine Wagner* edited by Anne Wilkes Tucker, 8–10. New York: Aperture Foundation; Houston: The Museum of Fine Arts, Houston.

Mulcahy, Dianne, Ben Cleveland, and Helen Aberton. 2015. "Learning Spaces and Pedagogic Change: Envisioned, Enacted and Experienced." *Pedagogy, Culture & Society* 23 (4): 575–95. https://doi.org/10.1080/14681366.2015.1055128.

NACEP (National Alliance of Concurrent Enrollment Partnerships). n.d. "What Is Concurrent Enrollment." Accessed November 30, 2020. http://www.nacep.org/about-nacep/what-is-concurrent-enrollment/.

NASEM (National Academies of Sciences, Engineering, and Medicine). 2016. *Barriers and Opportunities for 2-Year and 4-Year STEM Degrees: Systemic Change to Support Students' Diverse Pathways*. Washington, DC: The National Academies Press. https://doi.org/10.17226/21739.

NASEM (National Academies of Sciences, Engineering, and Medicine). n.d. "Roundtable on Systemic Change in Undergraduate STEM Education." Accessed December 7, 2020. https://www.nationalacademies.org/our-work/roundtable-on-systemic-change-in-undergraduate-stem-education.

NASEM (National Academies of Science, Engineering, and Medicine). 2020. *Recognizing and Evaluating Science Teaching in Higher Education: Proceedings of a Workshop—in Brief*. Washington, DC: The National Academies Press. https://doi.org/10.17226/25685.

NCES (National Center for Education Statistics). 2019a. "Digest of Education Statistics." https://nces.ed.gov/programs/digest/.

NCES (National Center for Education Statistics). 2019b. "Profile of Undergraduate Students: Attendance, Distance and Remedial Education, Degree Program and Field of Study, Demographics, Financial Aid, Financial Literacy, Employment, and Military Status: 2015-16." US Department of Education, January. https://nces.ed.gov/pubs2019/2019467.pdf.

Neumann, Anna. 2009. *Professing to Learn: Creating Tenured Lives and Careers in the American Research University.* Baltimore: Johns Hopkins University Press.

NRC (National Research Council). 2015. *Reaching Students: What Research Says About Effective Instruction in Undergraduate Science and Engineering.* Washington, DC: The National Academies Press.

NSEC (Network of STEM Education Centers). Accessed June 28, 2020. https://serc.carleton.edu/StemEdCenters/index.html.

Otterbein University. 2019. "Cohort of Columbus City Schools Alumni to Graduate from Otterbein University Sunday." April 24, 2019. https://www.otterbein.edu/news/cohort-of-columbus-city-schools-alumni-to-graduate-from-otterbein-university-sunday/.

Pekrun, Reinhard, Anne C. Frenzel, Thomas Goetz, and Raymond P. Perry. 2007. "The Control-Value Theory of Achievement Emotions: An Integrative Approach to Emotions in Education." In *Emotions in Education*, edited by Paul A. Schutz and Reinhard Pekrun. Burlington, MA: Academic Press.

Piaget, Jean. 1971. *Psychology and Epistemology: Towards a Theory of Knowledge.* New York: Grossman.

Pinkerton, Byrd. 2016. "Wax Tablets, Chicken Rustling and the Medieval Roots of the Modern University." NPR ED, April 5, 2016. https://www.npr.org/sections/ed/2016/04/05/472139919/wax-tablets-chicken-rustling-and-the-medieval-roots-of-the-modern-university.

Plank, Kathryn M. 2019. "Intersections of Identity and Power in Educational Development." *New Directions for Teaching and Learning* 159 (Fall 2019): 85–96. https://doi.org/10.1002/tl.20351.

Prison Studies Project. n.d. "Why Prison Education." Accessed December 26, 2020. https://prisonstudiesproject.org/why-prison-education-programs/.

Public University Honors. 2019. "Estimated Class Sizes: More Than 90 National Universities." Last modified September 15, 2019; accessed November 29, 2020. https://publicuniversityhonors.com/2015/10/20/estimated-class-sizes-more-than-90-national-universities/.

Quinlan, Kathleen. 2016. "How Emotion Matters in Four Key Relationships in Teaching and Learning in Higher Education." *College Teaching* 64 (February 4): 1–11. https://doi.org/10.1080/87567555.2015.1088818.

Reinholz, Daniel L., and Naneh Apkarian. 2018. "Four Frames for Systemic Change in STEM Departments." *International Journal of STEM Education* 5, no. 1 (February 9). https://doi.org/10.1186/s40594-018-0103-x.

Sagy, Ornit, Yotam Hod, and Yael Kali. 2019. "Teaching and Learning Cultures in Higher Education: A Mismatch in Conceptions." *Higher Education Research & Development* 38, no. 4 (June 7): 849–63. https://doi.org/10.1080/072943 60.2019.1576594.

Sathy, Viji. n.d. "Visualizing Inclusion in the Classroom." Accessed December 7, 2020. https://sites.google.com/view/vijisathy/classroom-photography.

Schon, Donald A. 1983. *The Reflective Practitioner: How Professionals Think in Action.* New York: Basic Books.

Scott, Debra Leigh. 2020. "There Is No Such Thing as an Adjunct Professor." *The Homeless Adjunct*, April 18, 2020. https://junctrebellion.wordpress.com/2020/04/18/there-is-no-such-thing-as-an-adjunct-professor/. Also published by Adjunct Nation, https://www.adjunctnation.com/2018/10/22/there-is-no-such-thing-as-an-adjunct-professor/.

Shakur, Fayemi. 2018. "Dawoud Bey: 40 Years of Photos Affirming the 'Lives of Ordinary Black People.'" *New York Times*, December 24, 2018. https://www.nytimes.com/2018/12/24/lens/dawoud-bey-seeing-deeply.html.

Shor, Ira, and Paulo Freire. 1987. *A Pedagogy for Liberation: Dialogues on Transforming Education.* Westport, CT: Bergin & Garvey.

Shulman, Lee S. 1993. "Teaching as Community Property: Putting an End to Pedagogical Solitude." *Change: The Magazine of Higher Learning* 25, no. 6 (December 1): 6–7. https://doi.org/10.1080/00091383.1993.9938465.

Shulman, Lee S. 2004. *The Wisdom of Practice: Essays on Teaching, Learning, and Learning to Teach*, edited by Suzanne M. Wilson. San Francisco: Jossey-Bass.

Sontag, Susan. 1977. *On Photography.* New York: Farrar, Straus and Giroux.

Spirn, Anne Whiston. 2008. *Daring to Look: Dorothea Lange's Photographs and Reports from the Field.* Chicago: University of Chicago Press.

Springborg, Martin. 2013. "Teaching and Learning: Visualizing Our Work." *Thought & Action: The NEA Higher Education Journal* 29 (Fall): 141–50.

Springborg, Martin, and Cassandra V. Horii. 2016. "Toward a New Creative Scholarship of Educational Development: The Teaching and Learning Project and an Opening to Discourse." *To Improve the Academy* 35 (2): 197–221. http://dx.doi.org/10.3998/tia.17063888.0035.210.

Stolzenberg, Ellen Bara, Kevin Eagan, Hilary B. Zimmerman, Jennifer Berdan Lozano, Natacha M. Cesar-Davis, Melissa C. Aragon, and Cecilia Rios-Aguilar. 2019. "Undergraduate Teaching Faculty: The HERI Faculty Survey 2016–2017." Los Angeles: Higher Education Research Institute, UCLA. https://www.heri.ucla.edu/monographs/HERI-FAC2017-monograph.pdf.

Stoltzfus, Jon R., and Julie Libarkin. 2016. "Does the Room Matter? Active Learning in Traditional and Enhanced Lecture Spaces." *CBE—Life Sciences Education* 15, no. 4 (Winter): 15:ar68, 1–10. https://doi.org/https://doi.org/10.1187/cbe.16-03-0126.

Strijbos, Jan-Willem, Paul A. Kirschner, and Rob L. Martens, eds. 2004. "CSCL in Higher Education? A Framework for Designing Multiple Collaborative Environments." In *What We Know about CSCL and Implementing It in Higher Education*, vol. 3, Computer-Supported Collaborative Learning Series, 3–30. Springer Netherlands.

Sturdevant, Lori. 2020. "Minnesota's Higher Education Is Facing a Crisis." *Minnesota Star Tribune*, May 29, 2020. https://www.startribune.com/minnesota-s-higher-education-is-facing-a-crisis/570880262/.

Sutherland, Kathryn A. 2015. "Precarious but Connected: The Roles and Identities of Academic Developers." *International Journal for Academic Development* 20 (3): 209–11. https://doi.org/10.1080/1360144X.2015.1066343.

Talanquer, Vicente, and John Pollard. 2017. "Reforming a Large Foundational Course: Successes and Challenges." *Journal of Chemical Education* 94 (12): 1844–51. https://doi.org/10.1021/acs.jchemed.7b00397.

Talbert, Robert, and Anat Mor-Avi. 2019. "A Space for Learning: An Analysis of Research on Active Learning Spaces." *Heliyon* 5 (12): e02967. https://doi.org/10.1016/j.heliyon.2019.e02967.

Tamborini, Christopher R., ChangHwan Kim, and Arthur Sakamoto. 2015. "Education and Lifetime Earnings in the United States." *Demography* 52, no. 4 (August): 1383–407. https://doi.org/10.1007/s13524-015-0407-0.

Taparia, Hans. 2020. "The Future of College Is Online, and It's Cheaper." *The New York Times*, May 25, 2020. https://www.nytimes.com/2020/05/25/opinion/online-college-coronavirus.html.

Tate. n.d. "Documentary Photography." Art Terms: Tate's online glossary. https://www.tate.org.uk/art/art-terms/d/documentary-photography.

Terrassa, Jacqueline. 2018. "What is the 'Work'?" In *Seeing Deeply,* by Dawoud Bey, 193–99. Austin: University of Texas Press.

Theobald, Elli J., Mariah J. Hill, Elisa Tran, Sweta Agrawal, E. Nicole Arroyo, Shawn Behling, Nyasha Chambwe, et al. 2020. "Active Learning Narrows Achievement Gaps for Underrepresented Students in Undergraduate Science, Technology, Engineering, and Math." *Proceedings of the National Academy of Sciences* 117, no. 12 (March 24): 6476–83. https://doi.org/10.1073/pnas.1916903117.

Tough, Paul. 2021. *The Inequality Machine: How College Divides Us.* Boston: Mariner Books, Houghton Mifflin Harcourt.

Trager, Ben. 2020. "Community-Based Internships: How a Hybridized High-Impact Practice Affects Students, Community Partners, and the University." *Michigan Journal of Community Service Learning* 26 (2): 71–94. https://doi.org/10.3998/mjcsloa.3239521.0026.204.

Trostel, Philip. 2015. "It's Not Just the Money: The Benefits of College Education to Individuals and to Society." Lumina Issue Papers, October 14, 2015. https://www.luminafoundation.org/resource/its-not-just-the-money/.

Tucker, Anne Wilson. 1988. *American Classroom: The Photographs of Catherine Wagner.* New York: Aperture Foundation; Houston: The Museum of Fine Arts, Houston.

University of Minnesota. n.d. "The Virtual Museum of Education Iconics." Accessed January 1, 2021. https://iconics.cehd.umn.edu.

Vikberg, Thomas. 2012. "Teaching an Introductory Course in Logic to Undergraduate Students Using Extreme Apprenticeship Method." University of Helsinki, Master's thesis. http://urn.fi/URN:NBN:fi-fe201204103214.

Vygotsky, L. S. 1978. *Mind in Society: Development of Higher Psychological Processes.* Edited by Michael Cole. Cambridge: Harvard University Press.

Weaver, Gabriela C., Ann E. Austin, Andrea Follmer Greenhoot, and Noah D. Finkelstein. 2020. "Establishing a Better Approach for Evaluating Teaching: The TEval Project." *Change: The Magazine of Higher Learning* 52 (3): 25–31. https://doi.org/10.1080/00091383.2020.1745575.

Web Accessibility Initiative (W3C). n.d. "Web Accessibility Tutorials: Image Concepts." Accessed October 30, 2021. https://www.w3.org/WAI/tutorials/images.

Weimer, Maryellen. 2002. *Learner-Centered Teaching: Five Key Changes to Practice.* San Francisco: Jossey-Bass.

Whitford, Emma. 2020. "Public Higher Education in a 'Worse Spot than Ever Before' Heading into Recession." *Inside Higher Ed*, May 5, 2020. https://www.insidehighered.com/news/2020/05/05/public-higher-education-worse-spot-ever-heading-recession.

Wiebe, Sean, Ellyn Lyle, Peter R. Wright, Kimberly Dark, Mitchell McLarnon, and Liz Day, eds. 2017. "Introduction: Life Writing While Writing Life." In *Ways of Being in Teaching: Conversations and Reflections*, vii-xii. Rotterdam: Sense Publishers.

Willers, Nathan. 2019. "Marketing Authenticity in Higher Education: The Role of Digitally Altered Images in College Admissions." *Inside Higher Ed*, June 25, 2019. https://www.insidehighered.com/blogs/call-action-marketing-and-communications-higher-education/marketing-authenticity-higher.

Winkelmes, Mary-Ann, Allison Boye, and Suzanne Tapp, eds. 2019. *Transparent Design in Higher Education Teaching and Leadership: A Guide to Implementing the Transparency Framework Institution-Wide to Improve Learning and Retention.* Sterling, VA: Stylus Publishing.

Witze, Alexandra. 2020. "Universities Will Never Be the Same after the Corona-virus Crisis." *Nature* 582, 11 June 2020, 162–64.

Wright, Mary. 2019. "How Many Centers for Teaching and Learning Are There?" *POD Network News*, January 2019. https://podnetwork.org/content/uploads/Wright_PNN_NoCTLs_Jan2019_update2pdf.pdf.

INDEX

A

academic staff 208–209, 228, 229, 235–236, 247, 284, 291–292
active learning 168–170
adjunct 169, 228, 234–236, 256–257, 264, 265
administrator/administration 228–229, 247–254, 247–258
aesthetics 122
affordances 174
associate's institution 35

B

bachelor's institution 35
back of the class 103–113
beauty 121–122, 127–128
belonging 104–105, 168
bias 207
breaching 168

C

Carnegie classification 35
centers for teaching and learning 8, 23, 60, 275–276
change agent 271, 272
change practice 271, 291
change strategy 271, 291
chaos 119, 127–129, 130–134

community-based learning 199–215, 222
concurrent enrollment 216–222
constraint 152, 167
consultation 25, 60, 291, 295
contingent faculty 228, 234–235, 236, 247–248, 256–257
COVID-19 182, 198
culture 134, 168, 272

D

desirable difficulty 93
disciplines
    humanities 35, 77, 189
    social sciences 35, 189
    STEM 35, 85
    technical/professional 35
disruption 122, 182–184, 198
doctoral institutions 35
documentary/documentary-style photography 2, 14, 200, 270, 283, 295
dual enrollment 216–221

E

educational developer 44, 236, 270, 284, 289
educational development 23–24, 60, 276, 289–291
exhibit 284–288

F

facilitation 87, 276, 289–290
faculty work 130
feedback 23, 276
flexible learning spaces 189–190
frame of the photograph 62, 114–115

G

gendered conceptions of work 53
graduate students 130
graduation 13, 54, 271

H

hack 170–172, 199
hidden work 228–232, 255–257
high-impact practices 199, 207
historical photographs 30

I

identity 87, 134, 206, 223
instruction paradigm 84–86
intentionality 189

L

lab 30, 148, 152
learner-centered education 84–87, 103, 104, 115
learning paradigm 84–87
learning spaces 152–153, 189–190
lecture hall 103, 153, 161, 170

M

making photographs, guide to 295
marginalized students 104, 168, 271
master's institution 35
messiness of teaching and learning 120–124, 128, 133, 174

N

non-tenure-track faculty 234–235

O

observation 33–34, 290, 295
online education 182–188
organizational change 270, 289, 292

P

paradigm shift 84–87
partnership
    institution/community 198, 206, 222
    student-faculty 85, 87
passionate thought 94
physical presence 167
power 84, 167, 272, 289
professional development 23, 60, 289–291

R

race 52–53, 104
reflection 2–4, 32, 34–37, 59–63, 82, 284
release form 59, 295
retention 93
risk 104, 128–129

S

scholarship
  of photographs and education 30–32
  of teaching and learning 54, 133
service learning 199–209
STEM. See disciplines
stereotype 24, 32
studio 161
systemic change 270

T

Teaching and Learning Project 2, 7, 13, 31, 35, 44, 59, 87, 120, 152, 174, 183, 228, 272, 284
technology
  laptop 87, 120, 175
  phone 174, 177, 183
  projector 103, 155, 174, 179, 185

U

unstaged space 189–194

W

workload 255, 257, 264

Made in United States
Orlando, FL
29 July 2022

20288130R00186